EDITH PARGETER:
ELLIS PETERS

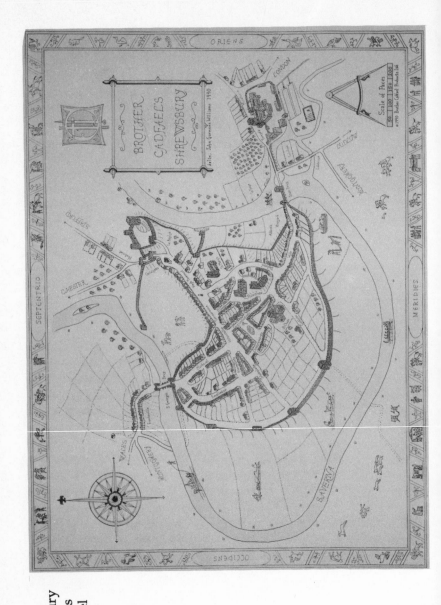

Fr. Map of Shrewsbury as envisioned by Ellis Peters for the Cadfael Chronicles

EDITH PARGETER: ELLIS PETERS

Margaret Lewis

Border Lines Series Editor
John Powell Ward

seren

To my family

Seren is the imprint of
Poetry Wales Press Ltd
Wyndham Street, Bridgend
Mid Glamorgan, Wales

© Margaret Lewis, 1994
Editorial and Afterword © John Powell Ward

A CIP record for this book is available at the
British Library Cataloguing in Publication Data Office

ISBN 1-85411-128-0
1-85411-129-9 pbk

*The publisher acknowledges the financial support of the
Arts Council of Wales*

Cover photograph by Talbot-Whiteman

Printed in Palatino by WBC Book Manufacturers, Bridgend

Contents

Author's Note	7
Acknowledgements	8
1. A Shropshire World	9
2. The Growth of a Novelist	21
3. The Czech Connection	34
4. Crime on the Borders — the Felse Novels	48
5. A Turbulent History	68
6. The Cadfael World	82
7. The Chronicles of Brother Cadfael	105
Conclusion	139
Bibliography	141
Series Afterword	147

List of Illustrations

fr. Brother Cadfael's Shrewsbury.

1. Edith's mother, Edith Hordley.

2. The Pargeter children: Ellis, Margaret and Edith.

3. Ellis Pargeter, sketched by Helen Trevelyan.

4. Edith's sister, Margaret, as a young woman.

5. Petty Officer Edith Pargeter, WRNS.

6. The Operations Room at Western Approaches Command Centre, Derby House, Liverpool.

7. Edith in Prague with Ravi Shankar.

8. The award of the Gold Medal and Ribbon of the Czechoslovak Society for International Relations in Prague, 1968.

9. 'The Bard', by John Martin.

10. Historical research is taken seriously.

11. Edith visits the set for the television productions of the Cadfael Chronicles.

p.87 A page from the Cartulary of Shrewsbury Abbey

Author's Note

Most contemporary readers of Edith Pargeter will have come to her books through a pseudonym, Ellis Peters. Yet half her literary achievement reached the public under her own name, Edith Pargeter. Recently some of these early novels have been re-issued as by Ellis Peters, using the name associated with her enormous popular success.

To avoid confusion, but to retain an accurate picture of the publishing history of this writer, I have referred to Edith Pargeter in the chapters which deal with novels originally published under that name. When she uses the name Ellis Peters, so do I.

I hope that this account of the life and work of Edith Pargeter will make readers aware of the scope and quality of her writing over nearly sixty years. The Chronicles of Brother Cadfael very properly receive extensive treatment, but her historical novels, her translations from Czech and her border detective stories are all discussed and are seen as part of a highly professional and dedicated career.

Acknowledgements

I am very grateful to Edith Pargeter for the interest she has shown in this book and for her patience in dealing with my many enquiries while it was being written. I should also like to thank her literary agent, Deborah Owen, and her editor at Headline, Lord Hardinge, for their assistance. Newcastle City Library, the Robinson Library and the Audio Visual Centre of the University of Newcastle upon Tyne, the Lit and Phil Library of Newcastle upon Tyne, and the National Library of Scotland have all been most helpful in tracking down rare and out of print books. Margaret Eve's sage comments and Barbara Sumner's computer skills have been invaluable.

ML

The author thanks Edith Pargeter for providing illustrations 1, 2, 3, 4, 5, 7, 8, 10 (the latter with Talbot-Whiteman of Leamington Spa). Acknowledgements for the other illustrations include: Western Approaches (6); City of Newcastle upon Tyne (9); Central TV and John Rogers (11); John Garnons Williams (frontispiece); the National Library of Wales (p.87).

Acknowledgements are also due to Edith Pargeter/Ellis Peters's various publishers. Quotations are reproduced by permission of Headline Book Publishing Ltd from its hardcover and softcover editions of *Warfare Accomplished, The Hermit of Eyton Forest* and *The Summer of the Danes*. Quotation from *Shropshire* is made by kind permission of Alan Sutton Publishing Ltd. Quotations from *The Fair Young Phoenix, The Grass Widow's Tale, The Scarlet Seed* are reproduced by permission of Little, Brown and Company (UK) Ltd. Quotations from *The Rose Rent* (1986), *The Virgin in the Ice* (1987), *The Pilgrim of Hate* (1990), *Monk's Hood* (1991) and *The Raven at the Foregate* (1992) are reproduced by permission of Macmillan General Books.

1. A Shropshire World

This earth is dense with days, lived through
and left behind in long-repeated seasons
                    'At Bywell', Lauris Edmond

Borderlands are lands of tension, where cultures clash and divi-
sions linger, creating uneasy reconciliation of dyke or wall. For
eight years the Emperor Hadrian laboured to keep the Scots at bay
by meticulously laying out his milecastled wall across the north of
England from the Solway to Wallsend. The wall still stands, a
physical symbol of violent confrontation that was to endure long
after the Romans had left Britain or intermarried and settled down
in these troubled northern provinces. When the last Romans had
departed from the western shores of Wales, the mountains assumed
a defensive position between Celts and Anglo-Saxons. Offa's Dyke,
dug out in the eighth century to separate England from Wales, can
still be followed, and, like Hadrian's Wall, establishes the principle
of division; a borderline of landscape and of mind.

The ancient county of Shropshire remains a borderland, should-
ering rough mountains to the west where Welsh place-names pre-
dominate but sloping gently eastward to the fertile fields of England.
The river Severn bisects the shire. Vital territory; this borderland
between Anglo-Saxon and Celt represents more than simply conflict
between truculent tribes. Throughout the centuries the Celts have
maintained their own language, poetry, music and religion. Evidence of Celtic Christianity lies even now as a hidden motif in the
landscape of Wales, with saints and holy places more revered for
wisdom and healing than the stern Anglo-Saxon gods of battle and
sacrifice.

Tactically alert, the eleventh century Norman invaders built their powerful defensive castles down the length of the border with Wales; Shrewsbury Castle is one of many such massive constructions. These castles were still of crucial importance as late as 1403 when Henry IV defeated the rebels at the Battle of Shrewsbury, a battle which drew Harry Hotspur from the northern borders in alliance with Owain Glyn Dwr on the borders of Wales.

Borders may signify conflict, but they also signify diversity. For Edith Pargeter, with a Welsh grandmother and English parents, the consciousness of such oppositions has directed much of her life and work. She is conscious also of her roots, writing in her book *Shropshire* that:

> The interplay between man and his environment affects the way he lives his life, the work he does and the way he does it. And Shropshire has left its images in my books as indelibly as in my memory and imagination. I am well aware that my writing is very visual, I paint in words. The landscape, the townscape, weather and season are all there within and between the lines... Shropshire is present as a pervasive sense of place, never fully revealed, but strongly felt. (p.159)

* * *

Edith Pargeter's earliest landscape was not of lonely, wind-whipped mountains, but the scarred banks of the river Severn, where in Coalbrookdale and Ironbridge the industrial revolution began. Born in the small village of Horsehay on 28 September 1913, and christened Edith Mary, Edith had an older brother, Edmund Ellis (born in 1907 and always called Ellis) and an older sister, Margaret (born in 1911). Their maternal grandmother, Emma Ellis, was Welsh, and lived with the Pargeters. She gave her maiden name to her grandson, and many years later, to her granddaughter too. Like most people living in the area the family depended on the local Horsehay Ironworks for a livelihood; her father was head clerk and timekeeper and later her brother also worked there as an engineer.

Edith remembers her mother, Edith Hordley, as being 'artistic, musical and interested in everything'. With three children, a husband and an elderly mother to care for in a two-bedroomed terraced cottage lacking electricity, gas or water she must have had little leisure time, yet her daughter will never forget the zest for life that she shared with her family and friends. She played the violin, wrote poetry, sang and read aloud to her children. She took them for long walks in the surrounding countryside, naming birds and flowers as they strolled through the ruined abbeys of Buildwas and Much Wenlock. 'The house,' said Edith, 'was full of books and music. Not very much else, but I don't ever remember feeling deprived.' All the children could read by the time they went to the village school in Dawley, a mile away from home.

The Pargeter children had as their playground the tired, yet rejuvenated landscape of eighteenth century industrialism. It was a world of contrasts. Here were streams and wildflowers but also ruins of forges long abandoned and huge mechanical devices left to decay. The river Severn, deep in its wooded gorge, could perfectly reflect Telford's famous iron bridge in calm waters, but it could also run tumultuously in spate — 'in the Severn gorge weather and season were aways exciting', Edith remembers.

Ironbridge Gorge, where Edith attended Coalbrookdale County High School for Girls, is now a World Heritage Site, the first British monument to be so recognised by the United Nations. When Edith walked up and down the steep slope between home and school she would have traversed two centuries of industrial history, beginning with Abraham Darby's 1709 blast furnace which used coke instead of charcoal to smelt iron. Ranged along the banks and up the hill were the later foundries and the houses of the Quaker ironmasters who developed the potential for cheap cast-iron products.

The circumference of her childhood world was limited in distance but rich in history — 'we made the most of our own county'. Abbeys, historic towns and iron age forts were the landscapes of her early years. The nearest county town was Shrewsbury, which as a young child she visited regularly with her mother to see an eye specialist about poor sight in one eye. Their days out in town were spent exploring the narrow medieval streets where half-timbered houses lean companionably towards their neighbours across the way. The turretted castle stands high on a loop of the river Severn; a fine position well chosen by the Norman barons to impose their strict rule on the defeated English shires after the Battle of Hastings in 1066. Rambling along the river bank or through the town from the abbey to the castle, Edith, as a little girl, was laying down in her mind the pattern of an imaginary twelfth century world.

Another landmark was the Wrekin, a volcanic hill rising dramatically from a flat plain a few miles from Shrewsbury. Although only

1,335 feet high, the abrupt rise of the Wrekin gives it a presence that belies its height. There is a spectacular view from the top looking as far as Derbyshire, the Cotswolds and the Welsh mountains. Such a vantage point was no doubt why an Iron Age fort was built here, the capital of the Cornovii, a powerful tribe that held the borders before the Romans pushed westward. Legends of battling giants surround the Wrekin. The traditional Easter Monday climb to the top of the hill made by the Pargeter family, in company with hundreds of others, may well have had a significance that goes back to these prehistoric times.

A more frequent trip was to the small town of Wellington, three miles from Horsehay, where her mother's brother, Tom Hordley, lived with his large family. This was an opportunity for the young Pargeters to play with their cousins, who were close to them in age, and to enjoy some convivial music-making. All the Hordley family could play some musical instrument (Tom played the accordian and the violin) and several sang well, although none took it up professionally. Edith's mother had a good mezzo-soprano voice, and sang a wide variety of songs from operatic arias to music hall ballads and folk songs. A lifelong pleasure in music developed as a result of these early impromptu home concerts, taking Edith in later years to the more eclectic realms of the Indian sitar and the Slovakian pipes; to medieval plainsong and opera. Many of these musical interests are reflected in her fiction.

Life remained very much based within a narrow radius during her early years. 'We never went on holiday, except occasionally to aunts or cousins for a treat. Few ordinary families did in the twenties; few could afford to,' Edith remembers. But she began to know Shropshire intimately, and wrote in *Shropshire* that:

> I have used this landscape, native and familiar to me, in all
> my books, sometimes in its veritable shape and by its own
> names, sometimes with its edges diffused into a topography
> between reality and dream, but just as recognizable, for those
> who know it as I do, as if it had been mapped with the
> precision of an Ordnance Survey sheet. I did not set out
> deliberately to make use of my origins. Shropshire is simply
> in my blood, and in the course of creation the blood gets into
> the ink, and sets in motion a heartbeat and a circulation that
> brings the land to life. (p.26)

A SHROPSHIRE WORLD

* * *

The growth of the writer emerged as naturally as her knowledge of the layers of history that surrounded her: 'I always knew I wanted to write.' From the age of five she was at work — 'the usual little verses at first, then stories all through school, just for myself. My sister and I both told stories, taking it in turn if we were doing something not very interesting, like dusting, or otherwise helping in the house. She was very good at it, but never wrote down anything or persevered with it'. Edith started her first novel at the age of twelve; at school she was known as 'the girl who never stopped writing.'

Edith was fortunate in having two teachers who believed in stimulating the imagination of their pupils, and who were sympathetic to her ambition to be a writer. In the last years of her primary school Mr Donald Wase encouraged her and as a scholarship pupil at Coalbrookdale High School for Girls Edith was helped by her English teacher, Miss Ethel Harvey, whom she remembers with great fondness. English, Latin and History were subjects in which she excelled. It must have been unusual for a fifteen-year-old schoolgirl to scrape together the not inconsiderable sum of five pounds to purchase the two-volume *History of Shrewsbury* by Owen and Blakeway that had been advertised in a local paper. The books are still on her bookshelf and are consulted when needed. On leaving school, Edith was well qualified to go on to university or training college had she so desired. But her pathway seemed clear and she was sufficiently strong willed to take it. Edith Pargeter was determined to be a writer.

When Edith left school in 1930 the economic and industrial heart of the Midlands was suffering the effects of worldwide recession. Work was scarce and she had to find the means to support herself, while still living at home. Eventually she found a post as assistant in a chemist's shop in the neighbouring village of Dawley, where she worked for seven years, using her spare time to write. Much of her knowledge of medicinal drugs came from this time, together with her background knowledge of nursing and first aid.

Fiction, once encouraged, seemed to flow from her pen. By 1939, when the Second World War began, she had published six novels, two under the pseudonym Jolyon Carr and one published as Peter Benedict. These had first been published in serial form in regional newspapers and later, slightly rewritten, as books. At that time regional newspapers often carried serialised novels and this provided her with an early foothold as a writer. The style was strictly controlled with thirteen instalments, the opening section longer than the rest. For an apprentice at the craft, following such a rigorous structure was not necessarily a bad thing, as it made her acutely aware of the devices involved in creating and sustaining a gripping narrative line.

The outbreak of the Second World War gave many single women an opportunity to leave routine occupations and join the forces. Edith was no exception and she tried to enlist in the WRAF but discovered that her job as a chemist's assistant was considered to be a reserved occupation and her services were needed where she was. The only solution was to resign and try again with the WRNS, this time listing her occupation as author: 'authors were clearly expendable, because I was accepted without question.' At the age of twenty-six she was leaving home, and Shropshire, for the first time, and was posted to Plymouth to work for Western Approaches Command, administering the Allied convoy route across the Atlantic. The Command subsequently moved to Liverpool where Edith stayed throughout the war, enduring night after night of ferocious bombing in May 1941, as the Luftwaffe attacked the docks. Edith was a teleprinter operator in the Signals Office with nine other women on her watch and monitored a direct trans-Atlantic line to Newfoundland. In 1944, Edith was awarded the British Empire Medal 'for zeal and whole-hearted devotion to duty.' The medal was presented on VE Day, 8 May 1945, when the war in Europe was officially declared over, and Edith celebrated in the streets of London with thousands of others. She left the WRNS in July that year with the rank of Petty Officer.

Being in uniform had not stopped her writing, and she published five more novels during or immediately after the war years, including a book about the WRNS, *She Goes to War* (1942), and a trilogy about the common soldier's war, *The Eighth Champion of Christendom*.

Perhaps growing up in a small house with a large family had taught Edith how to concentrate on her writing in unpropitious circumstances: 'I could concentrate in the common room, with table tennis at one end and someone playing the piano at the other.' By now, modest royalties were beginning to accrue from novels and from stories in magazines such as *Good Housekeeping, Everywoman* and *Argosy*. Edith returned to Shropshire and lived with her mother until her death in 1956; her father had died in 1940. She and her brother then bought an eighteenth century house in Madeley, about a quarter of a mile from where she lives now and they lived together for the next thirty-five years. Neither of them married; Edith has said that 'I found out quite early that I was much better at friendship than I would have been as a wife and mother.' But she does believe in what she calls 'passionate friendships between the sexes. They add a tremendous amount to life.' Although remaining a very private person, she values her wide acquaintance at home and overseas. Yet her career as a writer was always put first and she told June E. Prance in an interview in *British Digest Illustrated* that: 'I was a career woman before it was the done thing, and I have a feeling that our generation of women — especially after World War II — were the ones that broke loose from the mould — the traditional thing of marriage and children.' Pargeter recognised that, for her, an intensive creative life could not be combined with a full domestic commitment, and she continued to find emotional and creative satisfaction in her work.

Returning to Shropshire after the challenge of the war years was a decision that was to direct the future course of her life. She drew closer to her brother, finding much in common with his views and attitudes. They were members of the Workers' Educational Association (the WEA) and worked with others to establish the Shropshire Adult College at Attingham Hall, an eighteenth century mansion four miles south-east of Shrewsbury. After being relinquished by the army, which had occupied the building during the war, the hall and its Humphrey Repton garden was placed in the care of the National Trust. Part of the hall was leased to the proposed Shropshire Adult College — 'the fulfillment of a dream' wrote Edith — and with the distinguished historian Sir George Trevelyan as Warden, a huge effort was made to get the college underway. Working parties cleaned, painted and unloaded furniture. The co-operative effort brings back happy memories which she expresses in *Shropshire*:

> In some ways those first weeks, and the eventual opening, were the best days of all, as anticipation is always particularly fine when you are working personally for the end in view. Fees were kept low so that entry should be open to as wide an intake as possible, and under Sir George Trevelyan's magnetic and passionate leadership the college began an exultant life. (p.126)

There were weekend and summer courses on a wide variety of topics, with concerts, plays and poetry readings. But as with many such altruistic ventures financial pressures began to mount and Attingham Hall was forced to close as a WEA college, although it reopened in a different form a few years later. Edith still values the role it played as an adult college: 'I know that those years at Attingham opened windows upon an immensely expanded world for very many people, and I am sure nothing put into that co-operative has been wasted, or fallen without fruit.'

Edith has claimed that she was never political but strong positions are taken in many of her novels (particularly in the war trilogy) and she admits that 'when there is genuine feeling, a writer's politics will emerge of themselves. Politics, that is, in its widest sense, the art and ethics of living together in a society.' She made clear connections between international affairs over which she had no direct control and her own personal morality. An event which had affected her deeply was the Munich Agreement of September 1938, by which one fifth of Czechoslovakia was ceded to Germany in hopes of avoiding war in Europe. Hitler seized the remainder of Czechoslovakia six months later. Many British people were ashamed by their Prime Minister's betrayal of an ally, even in search of 'peace in our time', and Edith Pargeter was one of them. To her, the outbreak of World War II was a necessary reparation.

While she was in uniform she became friendly with many Czech and Polish airmen and made a firm decision to visit Czecholsolvakia as soon as she could. The opportunity came in 1947 when she and her brother took part in an international summer school near Prague. British and Czech people met and friendships were established that lasted for many years. Edith returned the following summer and stayed for three months. Her experiences are described in her book, *The Coast of Bohemia*, published in 1950.

From then on, Edith and Ellis visited Czechoslovakia regularly. Her friends and acquaintances extended beyond the original network of the 1947 Summer School and a growing interest in Czech literature brought her into contact with novelists and poets. Edith studied the bookshelves in her friends' houses and discovered that many nineteenth century Czech classics were unavailable in English. She set about teaching herself Czech so that she could make her own translations and has now published sixteen distinguished translations of poetry and prose, ranging from a life of Comenius

(1958) to contemporary novels.

During the 1950s Czech government restrictions made visits more and more difficult. From 1950 to 1956 it was virtually impossible to get a visa, but tourism was encouraged from 1956 onwards and once more Edith and Ellis were able to take the car for long summer holidays. As the government began to open doors to the West, Edith spent more time in Czechoslovakia.

During the 1960s she translated ten books as well as writing her own historical and crime novels. Her contribution to Czech culture was recognised in 1968 when the Czechoslovak Society for International Relations awarded her their gold medal and ribbon. Now her friends are able to visit England, where they seem amused to see rows of books in shops bearing the name that joins the Celt and the Czech: Ellis keeps alive the memory of her much-loved Welsh grandmother as well as being her brother's name and Peters is a variant of Petra, the name of the daughter of a Czech friend. 'They are a people I not only love, but admire,' Edith has said, and is able to feel herself as a Czech, 'with all their hopes and needs.'

As Edith's horizons broadened to Central Europe and beyond she continued to deepen her knowledge of eleventh and twelfth century history of the Welsh borders. A series of gripping historical novels emerged from her research, many of which had been established in her mind years before she began them. History, in Shrewsbury, is never far away, and it is not hard to keep the past alive when one walks regularly up the steep slope of Wyle Cop from the car park near the abbey, passing on the left the traceried window of Henry Tudor House where Henry VII reputedly stayed on his way to the Battle of Bosworth Field in 1485. The turrets of Shrewsbury Castle still guard the approaches to the town. A weekly shopping trip into the centre brings one to the market Cross where the body of Harry Hotspur was ignominiously displayed after the Battle of Shrewsbury in 1403.

By the early 1950s, Edith Pargeter had become established as a writer of contemporary fiction, often with a strong romantic flavour. Her readers were somewhat surprised, therefore, to pick up *Fallen Into the Pit* (1951) and find a modern detective story featuring a policeman, Detective Sergeant George Felse, and his family. Pargeter had used pseudonyms before to publish crime fiction (four novels as Jolyon Carr, one as John Redfern) and romantic fiction (Peter Benedict). The Ellis Peters pseudonym first appeared in 1959 with a non-Felse novel, *Death Mask*. Pargeter wanted to publish her major historical novels and her translations under her own name and the Ellis Peters pseudonym continued to be used for crime fiction from then on. Edith was able to sustain this multi-faceted approach throughout her career.

Pargeter's remarkable ability to categorise her fiction shows particularly clearly in the 1970s when a visit to India sparked off two Felse novels set there, while she was still keeping up the historical sequences that she was working on. The Indian friendships developed through connections made in Prague where she had become friendly with the Indian Ambassador and his staff — 'for three years or so, until diplomatic staff were moved on to new posts, we had a very pleasant Anglo-Indian-Czech private, if not secret, society.' She accepted an invitation to visit India, mainly in Delhi but also in the south. Her response to the sub-continent has been shared by many: 'I loved and hated India; the pressures of class division and riches and poverty there are devastating, but love predominates.'

In retrospect, the fusion of historical novel and detective fiction, the history and the mystery, seems almost inevitable, yet when Edith wrote her first book about Brother Cadfael, *A Morbid Taste For Bones*, which was published in 1977, she had no intention of continuing the series. Now, twenty Cadfael novels, plus short stories, have made her into an internationally best-selling author, with world-wide sales amounting to 9,800,000 copies. In all, over her prolific life as an author, Edith Pargeter has published over ninety books. Two novels have been broadcast on BBC Radio 4, *Monk's-Hood* in 1991, and *The Virgin in the Ice* in 1993. Four novels have now been televised by Central TV, and more are in preparation.

After the death of her brother in 1984 and two falls which left her mobility slightly impaired, Edith moved to a convenient modern house still very near to where she was born. Edith's cousin Mavis lives next door with her husband Roy Morgan, a retired architect, photographer and water colourist. Edith and Roy collaborated in producing *Shropshire*, published in 1992, a handsome celebration of the county in prose and photographs. They went on to publish *Strongholds and Sanctuaries*, another photographic volume about the Borders from Chepstow to Chester, in 1993.

Now in her eighty-first year, Edith Pargeter still finds herself drawn to the old portable typewriter on a small desk placed before her living room window. As she looks out over her tidily-landscaped garden, with the Severn gorge not far behind a border of trees, her mind is set free to wander in the less tidy paths of history that she has made so particularly her own.

Recognition from her readers and from her peers has brought bemused pleasure. In 1962 her Felse novel *Death and the Joyful Woman* was awarded an 'Edgar' for best novel by the Mystery Writers of America. The prize, a china bust of Edgar Allan Poe much coveted by many, sits in her house in Madeley, gazing with interest as monastic tales far removed from Poe's own grand guignol imaginings unfold beneath it. The English Crime Writers' Association awarded her a Silver Dagger in 1980 for *Monk's-Hood* and in 1993 she was given their ultimate accolade, the Diamond Dagger, presented at a ceremony in the House of Lords. She was given the OBE in the New Year's Honours List of 1994. In Wales, too, Edith Pargeter's work had not gone unnoticed. She was invited to join the Welsh Academy in 1990, an honour afforded only to 'a person who has made or is deemed to have made a substantial contribution to literature in Wales and/or to the maintenance of its high standard.'

Enthusiastic readers in the United States have coalesced around the Ellis Peters Appreciation Society, which was founded in 1989 by Sue Feder. It publishes a newsletter ('Most Loving Mere Folly') several times a year which gives reviews, factual material about life in medieval Europe and the occasional letter from Edith Pargeter.

American and English fans now mingle in the streets of Shrewsbury where they can follow in the footsteps of Brother Cadfael, or sit outside the abbey enjoying the fragrance from a new herb-garden which has been planted in his honour. Across the Foregate a new 'living history' exhibition, the Shrewsbury Experience, has opened. The Appreciation Society has sent donations to the Abbey Restoration Fund and has given financial support to install a new stained glass window to Saint Winifred near her shrine in the nave. Brother Cadfael souvenirs are on sale in the town, and a Cadfael rose bush (a fragrant, old-fashioned rose, with pink flowers) was introduced at the Chelsea Flower Show in 1990. Many readers were delighted by the publication in 1990 of *Cadfael Country*, a lavish photographic accompaniment to the novels with text by Robin Whiteman, photographs by Rob Talbot and an introduction by Ellis Peters.

Not for the first time, fact and fiction have blended and just as pilgrims from many countries make their way to the non-existent 221b Baker Street in London, sure that somehow the essence of that endlesly fascinating figure Sherlock Holmes will waft from a first floor window, followed by a fragment from a poignant violin, so they try to find in the busy streets of Shrewsbury the world of eight hundred years ago and the stubby figure of a pragmatic but humane Benedictine monk.

What they also find in all her novels is a profound sense of morality. In describing the kind of book that she choses to write, Edith has said in *Twentieth-Century Crime and Mystery Writers* that:

> It is, it ought to be, it must be, a morality. If it strays from the side of the angels, provokes total despair, wilfully destroys — without pressing need in the plot — the innocent and the good, takes pleasure in evil, that is unforgivable sin. I use the word deliberately and gravely. (p.848)

She is not afraid to celebrate goodness in her characters, nor to punish evil. But, like her creation Brother Cadfael, she is always alert to shades of grey, to the complex, mottled characters who make her novels so fascinating and ultimately so satisfying to a vast readership throughout the world.

2. The Growth of a Novelist

I am pocking the soil with my heel.
Here, here, here, here.
Into each footprint, a glimmering pearl.

They will not be counted,
these seeds, these stones, these
possible offerings from impossible language.
They resist being tears.

'A Dream of Stones', Anne Stevenson

Edith Pargeter's first eleven years as a writer show both a surprising diversity of fictional forms and growing maturity as a person and as a novelist. In the years before the outbreak of the Second World War Edith continued to work in the chemist's shop in Dawley and to write novels in her spare time. Fortune smiled on her first attempt at publication; 'I was launched rather easily', Peters told June E. Prance :

> A particular literary agent had put advertisements in several newspapers, saying that he was looking for talent. He planned to tour about four regional cities and was inviting anyone who had a manuscript that was fit for publication to come and see him. I didn't go to see him but I mailed him my novella and it was actually published. It was an extraordinary stroke of luck, not likely to happen today, I'm afraid. He was an unusual agent. He went out looking for good stories. He didn't just wait for them to come to him in London.

Between 1936 and 1947 she was the author of fourteen novels, using three pseudonyms as well as her own name. In 1937 she published *Day Star* as Peter Benedict and this was followed by four novels published serially in newspapers as Jolyon Carr: *Murder in the Dispensary* (1938), *Freedom for Two* (1939), *Death Comes by Post* (1940) and *Masters of the Parachute Mail* (1940). In the same year she published a crime romance, *The Victim Needs a Nurse*, by John Redfern. During this period she was also writing as Edith Pargeter, and it was under her own name that her wartime trilogy was published, bringing her substantial critical and popular recognition in the mid-1940s. She had changed her publisher to Heinemann in 1939 and stayed with them until 1963, although her crime fiction was published by Collins between 1959 and 1969.

Looking back at the beginning of her career, Edith Pargeter, like many writers, finds her very first books, especially the serial crime novels, something of an embarrassment — 'I confess I do shrink, rather, at the mention of those early pot-boilers, but of course I published them, so in the public domain they are.' At the same time she has the satisfaction of knowing that everything she has written gave her pleasure in the making, and she maintains that she never wrote any book 'out of calculation', even though the serialised novels did form a useful addition to the family budget at that time.

Certainly Edith's first book, *Hortensius, Friend of Nero* (1936), published when she was only twenty-three, grew from a fervent interest in the history of ancient Rome. She had emerged from school 'absolutely steeped in advanced Latin' and it is not surprising that this should have directed the subject of her first novel. The enthusiasm which lay behind its creation overcame many of the problems implicit in writing historical fiction: '*Hortensius* ran very rapidly and easily because of this special interest,' she remembers. It is a stylish and well-produced book, with illustrations by John Farleigh; clearly this new writer was being taken seriously by her publisher, Lovat Dickson. The prose is formal and decorative, verging at times on the prose poem as it tells the story of Nero's persecution of the Christians and his friend Hortensius's attempts to save them. For all its highly-wrought language — 'Our woods grow green and murmurous. Our rivers sing' — there is considerable dramatic power within the piece, a hint, perhaps, of a more direct confrontation with historical events which was to emerge in subsequent novels.

Her second novel, *Iron-Bound*, was also published in 1936 but could hardly differ more from her first book. If *Hortensius* arose from her academic studies, *Iron-Bound* took root in the world she knew, the iron works, the village and the pharmacy. The heroine, Bronwen

Clare (Brownie), works as an assistant in a chemist's shop and her father works in Thorpe Ironworks, as does her brother Tom. Brownie is a voracious reader and is hungry for knowledge and artistic stimulus. Her love of books brings her into contact with David Reid, the owner of the foundry. The novel is partly a doomed romance but also has a strong political and social foundation. The Lawrentian clash between the owner and the worker, what they tell each other and how they learn from each other, puts this novel into a category that transcends conventional romance. The long day of the shop girl, the walks in the rain because there is nowhere else to go, the consciousness of darned stockings and worn heels, give *Iron-Bound* an honest and credible feel. Pargeter claimed in a prefatory note that 'if there is a portrait in this book, it is the portrait of a district,' but that takes no credit for the delineation of character which shows a skilled observer at work. The melodramatic climax detracts from the novel's realistic approach but it still remains a considerable achievement for a writer at the outset of her career.

Plots ranging from events in ancient Rome to everyday workers in Shropshire, to film stars in the South of France indicate a writer obviously trying her wings. *Iron-Bound* was followed in 1937 by *Day Star* (written as Peter Benedict) which tells the story of a beautiful film star, Anthea Michaelis, who is told by a gypsy, 'you are a fatal woman — those who love you die', and indeed four men die, captivated by her beauty. Edith has cheerfully admitted that she knew absolutely nothing about film-making when she wrote the book but she researched the necessary detail to be able to describe film studios and film production with reasonable conviction. *Day Star* has a kind of escapist glamour that carries the reader along and again the portrait of the fatal woman and the effects of unrequited love have a quality that places it well outside the parameters of the familiar romantic novel. Edith would return to this theme with a different, more threatening, approach in her detective novel *The House of Green Turf* in 1969.

Edith Pargeter's first fictional encounter with the Second World War is in her novel *Ordinary People*, published in 1941, but written in the late 1930s. This book deals with a family of four children who grow up in the Midlands during the 1920s and 1930s, offspring of a strong mother and an amiable, unambitious father. There is little money to spare, and the children, who are all very different, learn early how to fight for what they want in life. The contrast between the parents, Ruth, who holds the family together, and George, who after returning from the rigours of the First World War never wants to leave home again, is sensitively portrayed. Unlike the Morels in D.H. Lawrence's *Sons and Lovers* neither parent is valued higher than the other and George, for all his lack of desire to seek advancement and give his family a better start in life, carries with him a rare sense of tranquillity and love. When he dies, his life shortened by lung damage caused by gas in World War I, it is as though the source of warmth in the family home has been lost. Ironically, at his funeral his youngest child Jason, an Oxford graduate and convinced pacifist, turns up in uniform, having joined up to fight a German army that is advancing once more across Europe. The cycle is seen to repeat itself, and in Jason, the reluctant soldier who has to cope with a conflict between abstract morals and a defence of civilised values, Edith was introducing a theme that grows in depth and sophistication throughout the four books she went on to write about the experience of war.

The Second World War had a profound effect on Edith Pargeter. In 1940 she left her familiar world of quiet Shropshire villages and her job in the chemist's shop in a local town and joined the Women's Royal Naval Service, the Wrens. As a practised writer Edith had learned to type, and familiarity with the QWERTY keyboard fitted her to become a teleprinter operator. She was posted first to Devonport, to the Signals Office of what was then the dual command, Plymouth and Western Approaches. But by February of 1941 it had become clear that far too many ships were being lost to U-boat attacks, and it was necessary to rethink the defences against this threat. The command was therefore split, Western Approaches HQ moving north, to Liverpool, the end of the main convoy route across the Atlantic. Many of the Wrens in Plymouth lived at home and came in daily, so it was natural that they should prefer in most cases to remain with the local command, while those who were mobile and lived in quarters went north with the Western Approaches staff under Admiral Sir Percy Noble. A special train transported them by night, through one or two sporadic air raids, to Liverpool.

There, in Derby House, a strengthened, purpose-built structure in Rumford Street, a highly integrated naval and air force command centre involving four hundred men and women worked around the clock to direct the Battle of the Atlantic. Information about the location of allied and enemy ships, submarines and aircraft was fed into the control centre at Derby House and processed, together with weather reports. Convoys out in the Atlantic were represented by wooden pieces moved around on a gigantic map of the ocean. It is hard to imagine the feelings of the Wrens who were ordered to remove a piece. Nearly two thousand allied ships were sunk in the Battle of the Atlantic and the loss of one ship, one piece from the board, could mean the death of over a thousand men.

She Goes to War, published in 1942, is close to Edith's experiences at that time: 'as far as the background is concerned, it is straight reporting.' She chose to use epistolary style and the novel consists mainly of the letters written by a serving Wren, Catherine Saxon, to an old friend, a crippled First World War pilot, Nick Crane. Edith says that she chose the letter form so that Catherine could speak for herself, openly, to someone she completely trusted. It was also appropriate for a time when letters were a crucial, and often the only, form of communication. Even then there was no guarantee that letters posted in wartime would arrive safely. Bombs fell nightly on British cities and convoys sailing to and from Britain suffered heavy losses. Postal deliveries, like many other services, continued under great difficulties. Inevitably the letter form suffers from a smoothing over of some of the raw material that Pargeter was attempting to deal with, but perhaps she needed a control mechanism to cope with experiences that included a bombing campaign where fifty thousand incendiary devices and 363 tons of high explosives were dropped on Liverpool on the night of 3 May 1941 alone.

The great strength of *She Goes to War* is that Catherine Saxon provides a view of war from a serving woman; a rare witness in the history of the English novel. As well as the professionalism lying behind the transmission of signals that helped to sink the German battleship the 'Bismarck' there is thoughtful consideration of how women behave when they are crammed together in one society (they form cliques) and how love can survive the artificial colouring given to it by long separations and snatched moments of intense joy. Catherine's friend Gwyn loses her handsome pilot fiancé who crashes into the North Sea after shooting down his thirty-third German plane. Yet as a wartime hero he will endure, transcending the mundane world of jobs and bank accounts that awaits these young men should they manage to survive the war. Edith herself saw many romances ended by telegram among the girls she shared quarters with, although she personally stayed clear of involvements:

'no romance, the war seemed to block out any such thought for me.'

The descriptions of nights spent in cellars while heavy explosives and incendiaries fall all around are particularly gripping because they are so understated. Night after night Catherine's friends pick up their knitting and books and file off underground :

> It's a funny sight we make, funny-ha-ha as well as funny-peculiar. Eighty or ninety girls in pyjamas, blankets, travelling-rugs, eiderdowns, greatcoats, scarves, their hair in curlers under giddy chiffon handkerchiefs, their faces greased and glistening with cold cream; and all these girls crammed into two or three small rooms and the wide tunnels between, in deck-chairs, on the floor, on top of one another, entangled in one another's knitting and embarrasssed by one another's books. Like a feminine jig-saw puzzle... (p.179)

Typically, the only hysteria arises from a large spider shaken down with some dust from the ceiling — 'you never saw a corner evacuated so quickly in your life.' Looking around her cellar, Catherine is pleased with what she sees: 'Sometimes I love my sex, Nick. I rather like them tonight. They're doing all right.'

Like Jim Benison, the hero of the war-time trilogy which followed this book, Catherine has joined up for no very precise reason, just a vague feeling that 'having been driven to the extremity of war against our will, let's not be ashamed of doing the thing thoroughly.' She drifts away from her fiancé, who did not enlist, and finds that she is becoming more and more critical of the black marketeers and civilian businessmen who are making huge profits from exploiting the situation. Describing the after-effects of the most devastating bombardment in May she indignantly tells Nick that the biggest hotel in Liverpool denied food to 'a bunch of wet, grimy, smoke-blackened AFS men who'd been fighting fires on the docks all night under heavy bombing. I vouch for this.'

But Catherine's war is not all negative. She meets Tom Lyddon, a veteran of the Spanish Civil War, and someone who shapes her tentative and undeveloped views of the political and social changes she sees as necessary in British society. His final letters from Crete, where he dies as the result of yet another bungled campaign, are full of sentiments that yearn for a new age, asking when they will be 'out of the shadow of the idea that government should be left to the elect by birth and training, still bound hand and foot by a theory of social discipline which died long ago and will never carry us through any ordeal again?' The novel ends with Catherine realising that her war extends beyond the struggle with Hitler and Mussolini, and German U-boats in the Atlantic, and is likely to last well beyond the cessation of hostilities:

> No, it will not be over when we march through Berlin. It ends only when we have cut away from our own national body all the inequalities and exploitations and snobberies and simonies and treacheries and embezzlements that enfeeble it now, and opened our frontiers to all progressive minds of whatever country and race without distinction; when we have assured not only for ourselves but for the whole world of men of goodwill the right to live in peace, dignity and happiness, as the brothers they should be. (p.312)

Edith Pargeter stayed in the Wrens for the rest of the war but she did not stop writing. There were major themes that took courage to embark on: 'Having written about my own experiences, there seemed nothing else worth writing about then but a man's war.' She and her colleagues worked under great pressure and were allowed generous time off. For Edith, relaxation was writing, and that is how she spent most of her free time. Her war-time trilogy is a remarkable achievement, 'written almost day by day as the events unfolded' and using material that came daily to hand. It is certainly the most ambitious piece of writing that she had achieved up to that time. War Reports in newspapers provided a basic account of the events of the war, and although these were much more informative than people now remember, they did not provide enough to sustain the detailed narrative that she had in mind. For this she turned to the seamen and airmen of many nationalities who passed through Liverpool during the war years. Her memories of that time remain vivid:

> We had visiting servicemen of a dozen nationalities in and out of the house, and, of course, our working base, since Poles, Czechs, Greeks, Scandinavians were all making their way to England to go on serving as their own countries fell victim. Seamen in particular came and went, and all with stories to tell. Again, as relatively well-off in our service quarters, we entertained fairly frequently, either the whole house or individual watches arranged parties; and since we had a military hospital just up the road, we always invited the walking

> wounded. Talk between people in uniform was completely
> free, though we never talked outside.

Edith was obviously a sympathetic listener and wherever she went she learned about what the common soldier had experienced. Leave trains, which often took many hours to reach their destination if there was an air raid in progress, were a rich source of anecdotes. Edith modestly says, 'Anyone who listened could have learned most of what I learned, though I drew on books for the countries that provided the background.' But listening, like storytelling, is an art, and Edith was clearly an expert at both.

The wartime trilogy gains much of its strength from its closeness to events. Two of the three novels, *The Eighth Champion of Christendom* (1945) and *Reluctant Odyssey* (1946) were being written during the last stages of the war while *Warfare Accomplished* (1947) was completed after the war had ended. In the fifty years that have passed since that time a number of fine works of fiction have been written about the war and its effects. J.G. Farrell's *The Singapore Grip* (1978), Paul Scott's *The Birds of Paradise* (1962) and J.G. Ballard's *Empire of the Sun* (1984) are examples. But there is a difference between fiction which is written after the event and uses the pressures and moral complexities of war to explore their reflection in contemporary society as Paul Scott does, and fiction which has the immediacy and, it has to be said, lack of polish that is part of a genuine proximity to history as it is being made.

Jim Benison, the ordinary soldier from Midshire (Shropshire) fights a very long war indeed. He joins up because he has a vague feeling that 'if the country's in a spot you can't sit back and look on — not if you're even half a man. If England's in trouble, so must you be.' That sentiment, and a desire for adventure, is enough to enlist him in the ranks of the 4th Midshires. His sentiments in 1945 are very different. He has seen many friends die, and many battles mismanaged. He has known the disheartening experience of retreating over ground that had been hard won with lives sacrificed from his own regiment. And perhaps hardest of all to come to terms with is the realisation that there is a huge gap between those who have had the experience of war on active service and those who have profited by the war at home. Class consciousness and snobbery, colour prejudice and bigotry now cloud his view of the England he wanted to protect. By the end of the war Jim is sharing the feelings of many servicemen and women at the time that English society needed radical change. These novels have a growing political edge that sharpens appreciably as Jim matures. Ending on a philosophical note, the trilogy is much more than a series of adventures. Jim Benison is reflecting the author's view, first expressed in *She Goes to War*, that post-war Britain needed to be a very different place in order to keep faith with those who had lost their lives during six years of conflict.

The Eighth Champion of Christendom deals with the first year of the war, culminating in the retreat from Dunkirk. The Midshires have been quartered for some time in the French village of Boissy-en-Fougères, where Jim has developed a deep and unexpected friendship with Miriam Lozelle, a Czech woman ten years older than him, who owns the farm where they are billetted. Later, retreating wounded and separated from the rest of his platoon after the disastrous advance to the Belgian border, Jim, rather too providentially, encounters his friend Tommy Goolden in the woods and both seek refuge with Mme Lozelle. Her efforts to see them returned to England result in her being arrested by the Gestapo, tortured and shot. Jim and Tommy set off across the Channel in a small boat but are machine-gunned and Jim, badly wounded, is the only survivor. When he returns home his fiancée has married someone else and Jim has moved a long way from his parents and his friends in the saloon bar of 'The Clay Pigeon'. Their comfortable platitudes about English invincibility ring very hollow to Jim, and he finds a kind of equilibrium finally in the shared experiences of Imogen, an old school friend who has been an ambulance attendant in London during the blitz.

The camaraderie that shapes the action of the first novel of the trilogy is developed much more fully in the second, *Reluctant Odyssey*, published in 1946, where Jim becomes a close friend of an awkward and anarchic member of his platoon called Charlie Smith. Charlie travels light and teaches Jim to respond to the space and beauty of the desert landscape of North Africa. Yet again Jim is involved in fruitless warfare ending in retreat: 'all they did was spar like a couple of terriers on a rubbish-heap.'

It is a very different experience when they are sent to Singapore. Pargeter was writing this novel in 1944-45, while censorship was still in place, but she was remarkably well informed about the débâcle that culminated in the surrender of Singapore. Even more interesting is her highly critical approach to the colony and indeed to the whole notion of Empire. Jim sees very clearly the fashionable hotels, the well-dressed, languid women and their stuffy English officers who regard the Midshires as drab but worthy: 'They were not, to the people of this city, equals, but only retainers. Except as a barrier against Japan, a kind of costly insurance, they did not exist.' Thinking back to the confused campaign in Flanders and that frantic retreat to Dunkirk, Jim is no longer convinced 'that all must go right for a cause in itself so right.' Not only does he now doubt the training and the command, he doubts the cause itself:

> Right will prevail, will it? It needs more than just the quality of being right. It needs tanks, and guns, and men, and realism in the use of them. You can be as right and good as you like, and remain hopelessly incompetent at running a war. And who could honestly claim that Britain had handled hers well? (p.89)

Pargeter is writing at her best in the description of the Midshire's desperate defence of the Malay peninsula. Taut and convincingly detailed, the episode is underpinned by Jim's anguished loss of faith in the cause but complete dedication to the men in his unit and his determination, somehow, to survive. Separated from the main body of the company they are captured by a Japanese raiding party and suffer hunger, thirst and ultimately arbitrary execution for those who cannot keep up with the rest. Charlie Smith is bayoneted in cold blood and dies slowly. Jim, although bound, savagely attacks the Japanese soldier who is responsible and manages to attract the attention of a nearby Australian platoon. Again Jim ends up escaping from occupied territory in an open boat, this time accompanied by a young Chinese nurse. Eventually he returns to England safely but it is an England from which he now feels increasingly alienated. Racial and class prejudice disgust him and the blatant profiteering that he sees all around make him no longer proud to be British. The simple Midshire road foreman has embarked on a sombre journey since he casually joined up in 1939, and like Catherine Saxon in *She Goes to War* he knows that the society he and many others come back to after the War must be shaped in a different way.

Warfare Accomplished, the third volume of the trilogy, is more episodic in style and suffers in comparison to the gripping adventure of the retreat from Singapore. Individual incidents stand out however, and more and more focus is placed on the way in which men work together and support each other as a team. Jim is now a sergeant; not the most popular rank, but one that carries considerable responsibility. By chance his company again finds itself in Boissy-en-Fougères where Jim has poignant memories of Miriam Lozelle, now regarded as a heroine and buried in the local churchyard. The return to Boissy allows the novelist to explore the interesting area of attitudes towards collaborators. Eliane, the beautiful daughter of the local bar owner, had flirted with Jim's friend Tommy Goolden and had also gone out with German officers during the occupation. The women of Boissy wait for their moment and seize it, administering the traditional punishment to women who are over-friendly with the enemy, shaving her hair and her eyebrows. Jim refuses to help her and uses the incident to educate headstrong young Teddy Mason into some of the grey moral shading of decisions taken in wartime.

The whole question of forgiveness and retribution is close to the surface of this book and it is approached from a number of angles. A young German girl who offers the advancing English tank regiment flowers is savagely dismissed by an officer, to the embarrassment of the men. Yet feelings of forgiveness are soon abandoned when they accidentally reach a concentration camp near Osnabruck. Jim's response to moral dilemmas is usually to force people to face up to the reality behind theoretical judgements and he draws considerable satisfaction from making the fur-coated wife of the camp commandant get on her hands and knees to scrub the floor of an empty barracks to house the wraith-like victims of starvation and disease. Any notion of acceptance of the innocence of German civilians is lost forever. Jim looks around him after leaving the camp in the less vengeful hands of the Red Cross and sees:

> ...everywhere in this countryside a sleek, servile, selfish, two-faced people keeping both eyes fixed firmly on their own advantage, and therefore unable to see any such open nightmare as the camp under the hill. If the fact of its existence was ever shoved pointblank under their noses they would swear they had no knowledge of it. No one could go near the farm, no one could walk over the hill without seeing the living skeletons ranging along the wire; but they would swear with tears their ignorance and consternation, and in some quarters, beyond doubt, they would be believed. (p.312)

The end of the war returns Jim to Midshire and to Imogen, allowing the trilogy to end on a note of qualified optimism about the future. He will never forget his murdered friend Charlie Smith's words about a future where passengers pay the full price — 'God help you if you let me down after this...dead or alive, I'll never leave you alone.' In July 1945 the Conservative government led by Winston Churchill suffered a resounding defeat. A strong Labour government responded to an overwhelming mandate to build a new society based on socialist principles. For a while, Edith Pargeter, too, had her hopes for the future. Reflecting now on the situation at the end of the war she finds that 'like most social explosions and most disillusionments with what we have, it went too far, and brought about a counter-disillusionment with what we put in its place. Somewhere there has to be a right balance, but our hopes overshot it in 1945. I suppose up to now they always have. So, yes, I suppose Jim's reassessment and Catherine's were also mine. Not repented later, but again reassessed.'

The war trilogy was very successful at the time and Edith has said that 'what pleased me most was that the serving men were their most enthusiastic advocates.' Their accuracy was also important to her and she was very satisfied when a War Office official told her that 'he had been through the third one to check on accuracy, purely as a matter of his own interest, and couldn't find any error worth mention in the account of the landings and the subsequent campaign.'

Contemporary reviews were extensive and, almost without exception, favourable: 'Her trilogy is a notable achievement' (*Birmingham Post*); 'a remarkable understanding of the soldier's mentality' (*The Scotsman*); 'Edith Pargeter gives continuous cause of wonderment' (*Books of Today*). Many reveal surprise that such realistic war novels could have been written by a woman. The reviewer for the *The Illustrated London News* said that 'As an outsider, I could detect no trace of a woman's hand in the actual war scenes. They are more thoughtful and continuous than most of their kind, from time to time suggesting, admirably, a bird's eye view; but they are not at all unreal or wavering.' *The United Services Review* of April 1947 observed that 'Miss Pargeter writes of war with the mind of a man, and she also displays a feminine intuition in peering inside the hearts and minds of her characters.' Ralph Straus, writing about the trilogy in the *Sunday Times* of 23 March 1947, found that "*Warfare Accom-*

plished is the third and last and also the most attractively exciting volume of Edith Pargeter's war-trilogy *The Eighth Champion of Christendom*... in the story of Sergeant Jim Benison a man's spiritual growth as he experiences the splendid as well as the monstrously ugly things of war is finely suggested. The sergeant may stand for all that is most solid and reliable in the British soldier...I can only repeat what I have said before: this is a quite astonishing book for a woman to have written.'

It is always the mark of the best writers that they are prepared to take risks. In writing her wartime trilogy from the male viewpoint, with imaginary details of that closed world and an attempt to understand the feelings of ordinary men in battle, Pargeter was stepping far beyond the territory that she knew and could be expected to write about. There may be occasional weaknesses in dialogue, in characterisation and in plot but overall the execution of these novels is confident and convincing. Her vision is broad enough to assess the society that has supported the war and the inevitable contrast between the comradeship of the soldiers and the social stratification still existing in the higher ranks. She sees the world her soldiers have come from and how changed they will be when they return. And she also explores the feelings and emotions of those who are tried to the utmost on many fronts. One or two reviewers complained that she had made her soldiers too sensitive, arguing that most sensitive men simply became numb in order to cope, but surely Pargeter's boldness in trying to get behind those masks deserves high praise. She brings together that sensitivity with a recognition of the excitement of battle and the positive features of men working together, deeply concerned for each other's survival. There is heroism, but there are no empty heroics in *The Eighth Champion of Christendom*. These novels should be much better known today.

3. The Czech Connection

'A fair young phoenix rising out of the pyre.'

The legacy of war stayed with Edith Pargeter for many years. After she was demobilised from the Wrens she returned to Shropshire but she was returning now as a well-known novelist, with a promising career opening up before her. Her world was expanding and in 1947, when the last volume of the trilogy was published, she was feted in London by her publisher, Heinemann. She became an interesting subject for newspaper interviews, not only for her opinions on fiction but as a result of her experience in the services. In an extended article in the *Sunday Chronicle* in March 1947 she spoke about women and their achievement in the Second World War, contributing to a debate that has continued since then about the role of women in society:

> By the time our particular base was closed down after VE Day it was being run almost entirely by women under the Admiral's immediate Staff. Women had discovered what they could do, and I suspect in most cases it was more than they had thought likely. They had discovered also what they could not do, and it was less than they had feared. Women could and can afford to acknowledge it. It is no longer necessary for them to assert that they are the equals of men; they know it to be true. Nor is this knowledge in any way a diminution of the stature of man, but a means to establish a new and better balanced relationship in which they shall both find their full scope.

Pargeter adds the more concrete recommendation that 'recognition of the principle of equal pay for equal work will help', and stresses that both men and women are going to need to adjust to the demands of the post-war world: 'the urgencies of peace...are no less than those of war, and ought to provide as strong a stimulus.'

The kind of stimulus that Pargeter envisaged presented itself later that year. Edith and her brother visited Czechoslovakia as part of an international summer school, organised in association with the WEA. There were at least a dozen such summer schools throughout Europe that year, held in most countries except Germany. Edith's group included lecturers from Birmingham University, who spoke about British history, culture and institutions. It was an experience which obviously changed her life. Deeply affected by the visit, Edith wrote a barely fictionalised account in *The Fair Young Phoenix*, published in 1948. The phoenix in this case is the Czechoslovak Republic, whose people were trying to rebuild the country after the damage done by the war, and the book is prefaced by a sonnet written by Edith, 'To the Czechoslovak Republic'.

After the serious and often tragic incidents of the war trilogy, *The Fair Young Phoenix* seems paradoxically both lightweight and passionately felt. It gives the impression of having been speedily written while the author was still overwhelmed by the experience she evokes and is less of a novel than a semi-fictional sketch. Even so, Pargeter's description of the assorted worthies from Midshire who travel by train to Czechoslovakia is amusing and perceptive. Councillor Crowe discovers good works in Czechoslovakia just in time for the local elections in his home town of Rilsford and his enhanced public standing as a result of his trip secures the desired result of becoming mayor. Mrs Falconer, who 'collected offices as small boys collect stamps or aircraft numbers, but perhaps more greedily,' and was always secretary to every organisation, is naturally included in the group, as is beer-loving Councillor Godolphin, who is automatically treasurer to the same organisations. Miss Phelps from the County Education Office has her eye on the mayor, for all her superior attitudes. Three teachers are included in the party of twelve, one of whom, Mary Thayer, is the character through whom the two weeks in Krasne Mesto are seen. Like the author, Mary's particular interest in Czechoslovakia begins in September, 1938, as she sits beside a radio while a Czech friend weeps to hear of the sacrifice of her country.

The train journey through Germany causes friction between Mrs Falconer and Mary Thayer and reveals Pargeter's continued preoccupation with guilt and atonement after the war. She is concerned by the easy sympathy that British people produce without thinking through to the political realities involved:

> Sunlight upon these ghosts of towns certainly fed the fires of the advocates of emotional pity; for half a mile or more along the track only shells of buildings standing, sometimes mere heaps of rubble, only here and there a single habitable room. They passed standing trains, bare and dirty, wooden-seated, crammed with pale, languid people who stared at them like sleep-walkers and gave no sign of seeing. And yet this picture could not be allowed to obliterate the picture of comparative prosperity in the country districts, nor the memory of other pallid ghosts, starved, mutilated, crowded together in Belsen, in Buchenwald, in Oswiecim, in Dachau. Both must be held in mind, and a balance kept between them; else the compassion was debased to a thing of unreason and injustice, and became a danger to a world instead of a strength. (p.12)

The argument between Mary and Mrs Falconer that has been brewing since the journey began finally explodes with Mrs Falconer convinced that Germany is sorry for the past and Mary resolutely sceptical — 'all that's wrong with the war, for them, is that they lost it.'

What makes this extended debate particularly interesting to a reader forty-five years later is that the issues were clearly alive and commonly discussed among the people that Pargeter describes. These are ordinary Midlanders facing up to the results of the war they supported. Mary argues strongly for the victims of German aggression who seemed at that time to be less likely to receive American aid than the aggressors themselves. She is accused of lacking faith in humanity, while Mrs Falconer is tartly advised by her opponent to cultivate some common sense. All the while the train is passing through the dreary ruins of many German towns and cities, where the population seems undernourished, demoralised and in poor health.

Pargeter has an excellent ear for the kind of ill-informed and self-satisfied conversation that takes place in pubs and railway carriages and which is often very revealing of the mood of the time. Her character Mary Thayer seems convinced that a new Europe needs more than soft-centred liberalism; she tells Mrs Falconer with robust emphasis — 'to forget what happened in the occupied countries is to lose half the knowledge from which we've got to make the future, and leave the whole picture out of focus.'

After this promising opening, the novel, if it can be called that, loses a great deal of its energy. Mary Thayer falls in love with Czechoslovakia where she finds everything to be admired, especially the speedy reconstruction of old towns damaged during the war. She becomes captivated by young Vit Svoboda, who is one of the Czech members of the summer school and is a student at Charles University in Prague. Although he is thirteen years younger than Mary they become inseparable, to the extent that tongues wag and Mary is warned to be more circumspect. Yet for Mary the close companionship of Vit enables her to understand the Czech people in a way that no official programme of lectures and tours could ever achieve. The two weeks come to an end with everyone apparently having gained something from the experience and genuine friendships established.

As a novel, *The Fair Young Phoenix* suffers from being a rather private and slightly indulgent book, with too much time being spent on the relationship between Mary and Vit at the expense of the development of the other characters. As an account of a unique experience, however, the book is full of interest and again displays Pargeter's talent to transform immediate events into fiction. Yet the nation that she visited in 1947 was already under threat, and the innocent romanticism of *The Fair Young Phoenix* was soon to be firmly crushed by Russian political power. A year later Edith visited Czechoslovakia once more, and wrote about what she found there, this time as a first-person, non-fiction account of her travels. The title of this book, *The Coast of Bohemia*, is a reference to Shakespeare's *A Winter's Tale* — 'Thou art perfect, then, our ship hath touched upon/ The deserts of Bohemia?'. There is, of course, no sea coast for hundreds of miles; Shakespeare's uncertainty as to the boundaries is perhaps an unknowingly percipient comment on the history of Czechoslovakia ever since. The book is prefaced by another of Pargeter's sonnets, 'To the City of Prague, for the Fifth of May'.

Once more Pargeter found herself an observer at history being made. She was meeting friends that she had first encountered at the summer school, yet the intervening year had seen radical political change in this country. Since the re-establishment of the Czech government under President Benes in 1945 a six-party coalition had been in power. In February 1948 a Communist coup took control. A month later the liberal foreign minister, Jan Masaryk, son of the heroic Thomas Masaryk, died in mysterious circumstances. In founding the Czechoslovak Republic in 1918 Thomas Masaryk had hoped to make his country a political and cultural link between West and East. Thirty years later, in June 1948, a Soviet style constitution was in place and all opposition was being eliminated. This, then, was the atmosphere that Edith found herself in, a puppet state on the brink of being totally subsumed by the USSR. Even so, she feels that 'no one had realized the enormity of what had happened in 1948, and I was unwilling to believe it could clamp down as it did...it took a little time to believe in what was really happening behind a landscape and cityscape virtually unchanged.'

Sir Cecil Parrott, who was in Prague after 1945, and later became British Ambassador to Czechoslovakia in the 1960s, described the three post-war years as 'a short semi-democratic breathing space before passing under another form of oppression in which much of what they had built up, or inherited from their great heroes of the past was destroyed.' Yet Pargeter was still optimistic in 1948, and wrote confidently that since her visit the previous year 'Czechoslovakia had achieved what amounted to a major revolution, and by some mental trick had been expelled by most English people to a limbo many thousands of miles from civilisation — which is, of course, confined to the areas occupied by those who think as we want them to think, and do as we consider they ought to.' The euphoria of individual citizens drew Pargeter into the shared hopes of that summer, and in *The Coast of Bohemia* she wrote positively that:

> I knew there must be considerable changes, of course; but that absolute change from white to black takes place only in the limited imagination, never in reality. Humanity remains obstinately human in spite of political distorting mirrors, whether they be coloured red, pink or true blue; and all things considered, I *do* like its face. (p.5)

But Pargeter soon came to see this period very differently. By the time *The Coast of Bohemia* was published in 1950, the sunny socialism of the summer of 1948 was already heavily obscured by threatening cloud. In 1968 she wrote an introduction to her English translation of Josefa Slanska's book *Report On My Husband* which looks back to the arbitrary arrests and show trials of 1951 and 1952. Pargeter comments there that such arrests and trials were already being used in 1949, and the Secretary-General of the Communist Party Rudolph

Slansky himself had put in place some of the procedures that led to his own summary execution. The value of *The Coast of Bohemia* lies in its contemporary witness to events that were still historically fluid. The three euphoric years since the end of German occupation were short but significant in trying to re-establish a democratic republic. Thomas Masaryk had written, 'Democracy is discussion', but soon his books, which could clearly be construed as anti-Marxist, were proscribed. When Mary Thayer in *The Fair Young Phoenix* is brought to see the reconstructed school in the town they are visiting, Krasne Mesto, busts of former President Masaryk, decorated with flowers, are everywhere. But for two decades afterwards Masaryk was excised from the history books, and a whole generation grew up deprived of the sense of identity that any nation finds in its past. By the early 1950s even good King Wenceslas, the Bohemian prince who championed the poor, cut down gallows and destroyed jails, was being described by Communist historians as an autocrat struggling to reinforce the feudal order with the support of the Catholic Church and Germany. Not until the late 1960s was Czechoslovakia able to emerge into the light once more, with some degree of intellectual freedom, short-lived though Alexander Dubcek's Prague Spring of 1968 was to be.

Meanwhile, in a quiet house in Shropshire, Edith Pargeter continued to translate Czech poems, stories and novels into English, done initially entirely for herself: 'I was just curious about the classics all my friends had on their shelves, and for most no translation existed, so with gramophone records and a grammar book I set out to make my own.' At first she translated poetry, and this led to two anthologies in subsequent years, *A Handful of Linden Leaves* (1958) and *The Linden Tree* (1962), as well as a special edition of a long nineteenth century poem, *May* by Karel Hynek Macha, in 1965. Translating Czech poetry was far from simple, as Edith has explained in an article she wrote for the *Bulletin of the Welsh Academy*:

> Merely contriving to read word by word was not enough; I needed a presentable English text in order to enjoy something of the experience of reading the original. The language is strictly phonetic, strongly condensed, but very rich in double and even treble rhymes. I cannot translate free verse, I need a formal skeleton to clothe. The more complex the rhythm and rhyme, the better. Sonnets are a joy. The more puzzle, the more pleasure.

It was while reading her translations of Czech poetry in the Philosophical Faculty of Charles University in Prague in the 1950s that Edith first met the writer and translator Zora Wolfova, and an enduring friendship began. Other writers got to know her at that time and she began to acquire a high reputation as a translator of poety and prose.

But with her profound belief in the ability of the Czech people to survive as a nation, it is not surprising that her first published book of translations from Czech into English was a volume of short stories by Jan Neruda. *Tales of the Little Quarter* is a Czech classic ('You would have hard work to find a Czech household which posseses no copy of it', wrote Pargeter in her introduction) and this 1957 London publication brought Neruda to many readers who had never been introduced to his bittersweet tales of life in the old streets of Prague. Pargeter took a year to translate the book and when it was complete she showed it to her then publisher, Heinemann. To her surprise they agreed to publish it, and the volume became a considerable success. *The Times* praised her translation highly, saying that, 'Miss Edith Pargeter has done English readers a great service in her version of Neruda's *Tales of the Little Quarter*'. Their review goes on to say that 'no journeyman translator could have given this beloved Czech storybook the English it deserved; Miss Pargeter, a novelist of distinction, does not fail her author.' And BBC Woman's Hour saw the political importance of her translation by pointing out that 'Edith Pargeter has translated these famous tales of his quite marvellously and she has done us a great service in reminding us of the indestructible tradition rooted in the small countries that lie behind the Iron Curtain.' In Neruda Pargeter found all the qualities she admired in Czechoslovakia and she wrote in her introduction:

> Out of his love for the Little Quarter he made a book the image of himself, high-spirited, amusing, compassionate, occasionally startling us by a flavour of astonishing bitterness, but having as its heart and ground an uncompromising affirmation that life, bitter and sweet together, is to be accepted with ardour, and humanity, in all its folly and imperfection, to be loved without reserve. (p.vii)

After successfully publishing Neruda in England, Pargeter was sought after by the Writers' Union to continue translating Czech works, especially those that they considered to be attractive to

Western readers. Her connections were with the Writers' Union and with the publishers Artia, who had to maintain their political credibility with considerable deftness of footwork. 'I was continually walking a tight-rope,' said Edith, 'in order to avoid harming people I wanted only to serve.' The English editor of Artia, George Theiner, who was long associated with Amnesty International and the magazine *Index on Censorship*, became a close friend, particularly after the military repression of 1968 when he left Czechoslovakia and moved to England. Other well-known writers who knew her included Dr Bretislav Hodek, translator of Shakespeare and author of the newest English and Czech dictionary, Arnost Lustig, the famous Jewish writer now living in the United States, and Dr Jiri Hajek, who was at one time Czech Ambassador to Great Britain and among the most eminent of the group of dissidents and intellectuals who founded Charter 77 in January 1977. Edith had made many friends in the Czech literary world at a time when trustworthy contacts in the West were cherished; her friend Zora Wolfova remembers that 'she was always careful not to endanger her friends, and discreet. It was a great encouragement for us who knew her that she was visiting our country even in the difficult times and helped us to be in touch with English culture and life...the writers were grateful when she decided to translate their works as her translations were very good and opened the way for Czech books abroad.' Edith had the highest respect for the writers she encountered: 'Most of the writers and people working in the book world there were fine, honourable people working under extreme difficulties. There were plenty of the other, opportunist kind around to make their lives hell. Even if co-operation with them hadn't made it possible for me, discreetly, to continue visiting and seeing my friends, I should have been happy to work with the best of them. And they were glad to meet and talk to an (approved) English person.'

In 1958 Pargeter translated two difficult works: *Don Juan*, by Josef Toman, over four hundred pages of highly decorated prose, again published by Heinemann, and Frantisek Kozik's book *The Sorrowful and Heroic Life of John Amos Comenius*. Dr Kozik himself requested that Edith translate this popular work. The book was lavishly produced by the State Educational Publishing House in Czechoslovakia. It was handsomely bound in linen with good paper and attractive line drawings to illustrate the text. Clearly a political statement was being made, since this great seventeenth century Czech figure, teacher, writer, reformer of education, friend of the poet John Milton and the intellectual Queen Christina of Sweden was nevertheless acceptable to the prevailing brand of Marxist historian. Comenius, who died in 1670, had been famous throughout the civilised world and was a figure whom Pargeter could wholeheartedly admire. At a time of great unrest and religious persecution in Europe he had maintained his faith in the future of society, saying that, 'It is needful that all nations should devote their powers to the common good, that they should seek peace and truth, and sow love among neighbours.' He was invited to visit London in 1641 by a group of Parliamentarians including John Pym and John Milton who wanted to hear his theories on universal knowledge. For a writer such as Pargeter, his views on individual freedom and the role of education were as valid in the 1950s as they had been three centuries earlier.

More translations followed in the 1960s and in each one the writer's tone is skilfully adapted to the text. Styblova's bleak novel *The Abortionists* (1961) is coldly analytical and highly-charged emotionally; both qualities emerge in the translation. In contrast, Bozena Nemcova's *Granny* (1962), a great favourite in Czechoslovakia for its peasant wisdom, is warm and cosy in tone. This book, which was first published in 1855, became the most widely-read classic of Czech literature, and the 1962 edition was published to commemorate the centenary of the author's death. In the same year Pargeter translated *The Terezin Requiem* for Heinemann, a short but powerful narrative by Josef Bor which describes the famous conductor Raphael Schachter's performance of Verdi's 'Requiem' given in the presence of Eichmann in the Terezin camp. Imprisoned here were some of the finest Jewish musicians of Europe. They were waiting for the completion of Eichmann' s new and efficient death camp at Auschwitz, where up to ten thousand bodies could be cremated in twenty four hours. After the performance the musicians were all sent there:

> The Command had promised that Schachter's company should not be separated. The promise was kept. All together they ascended into the first wagons of the first transport.

Pargeter's English version of this extraordinary event is brilliant; both passionate and controlled. Josef Bor had 'practically insisted' on Edith doing the translation, and she felt strongly that the story must be told as widely as possible. American publication with Knopf was secured the following year.

During the 1960s Edith was able to visit Czechoslovakia annually, often accompanied by her brother, who drove them all the way from Shropshire, with Edith doing the navigating. The visa problems of the 1950s, when applications were never refused, but on the other hand were so delayed that the applicant eventually had to give up, were over. The government realised that hard currency could be earned from overseas publication and also by having English translations of Czech classics for visitors to buy. Edith presented no currency problems as she left her earnings in Czechoslovakia to pay for her holidays. Her knowledge of Czech and Slovak music grew alongside her knowledge of the literature. Edith has said that 'the Czechs are possibly the most genuinely musical people in Europe, and the richness of their classical work is matched by the astonishing wealth and beauty of their folk music.' *The Piper on the Mountain* (1966), a Felse novel set in Czechoslovakia, was a fictional celebration of these qualities.

Gradually the demand for translation began to extend in the other direction from Czechoslovakia to England as Pargeter's own writing was translated by her Czech colleagues and made available to a reading public hungry for works from the West. One of her first works to be translated by Zora Wolfova was a short story, 'All Soul's Day' (later published in the collection *The Lily Hand*), which was printed in an early issue of *Svetova Literatura*, edited by the novelist and publisher Josef Skvorecky. Now her work is widely translated and includes *The Heaven Tree* trilogy as well as the Felse novels and, becoming increasingly popular, the Chronicles of Brother Cadfael.

By 1968 artistic innovation was once more flourishing in Czechoslovakia. During the 1960s a new generation of writers emerged, including Bohumil Hrabal, Vaclav Havel, Ivan Klima, Milan Kundera and Ludvik Vaculik. Otto Ulc wrote in his book *Politics in Czechoslovakia* that these writers 'represented a force challenging simplistic socialist realism as the recipe for cultural creativity. This new wave also contributed to the rehabilitation of the writer's profession...as in the Czech national awakening in the nineteenth century, the artists once again assumed the political role of articulating the demands of the citizenry'. (p.109)

As in Poland, many talented young people found stimulus in the film studios, where a new style of film was emerging, carefully treading a narrow path between political rigour and free expression.

One of the first Czech films to be shown and enjoyed in the West was *Closely Observed Trains* made by Jiri Menzel in 1966. It was based on a short novel by Bohumil Hrabal, *A Close Watch on the Trains*, which Pargeter translated for Cape in 1968. The deceptive simplicity of Hrabal's style, with his tongue in cheek humour, was not easy to translate but Pargeter was delighted to be asked to do it as she admired him very much. Young Milos is an unexpected hero, as is his grandfather, who tries to stop the advancing German tanks by hypnotizing them. For once the film was considered to be as much an artistic success as the novel and although Edith had nothing to do with the film she was very pleased with the result — 'it was of great interest to me, as I was familiar with the actors' names and qualities by then, and loved it'.

The heady political reforms instigated by Alexander Dubcek and his colleagues in 1968 and the moves towards 'socialism with a human face' that seemed to be within reach were propelled forward by writers, journalists and artists. The Writers' Union was the most powerful of the artists' unions and their Fourth Congress held in June 1967 had provided a platform for writer after writer to denounce government policies. This contributed directly to the downfall of Novotny's government and his replacement by Dubcek. The influential journal of the Writers' Union, *Literarni Listy*, with a weekly publication of 300,000 copies, represented a daring challenge to outmoded Russian-style communism. When censorship was lifted in 1968 there was an outpouring of literary work, and contacts with the West brought a wave of intellectual and artistic excitement that was felt throughout Europe. English publishers, inspired by the new liberal climate, began to take a serious interest in Czech and Slovak writers.

The sense of celebration extended to Edith Pargeter, and in the spring of that year she was presented with the Czechoslovak Society for International Relations Gold Medal and Ribbon at a luncheon held in her honour in the Prague Writers' Club of the Union of Czechoslovak Writers. Edith remembers the euphoria of the moment:

> I have never, in any place at any time, known a people so absolutely united, young, old, intellectuals, students, factory workers, miners; never known an atmosphere of such purposeful and radiant joy. For me that was literally something

new under the sun. Even after the threats began, and the danger was apparent, this marvellous unity was sustained. On Vaclavske Namesti I watched an elegant old lady stop to buy the defiant paper the students were printing and distributing, and when the boy thanked her, she responded with the most beautiful, proud smile,'No! *We* thank *you!*'

Yet at that time the clouds were already gathering, and immediately afterwards began the weeks of tension and menace, as Russia's reaction to the liberalisation became more and more ominous. Finally, in July, came the meeting on the Slovak border at Cierná, where the parties separated apparently peacefully. No one supposed that the crisis was genuinely over, but it did seem that it was postponed for a breathing space. Edith returned to Czechoslavakia in the summer for her usual holiday, and although the political atmosphere was tense, moves towards reform were still in place. A week after Pargeter returned to England, Russian tanks were crossing the border.

The Russian invasion of August 1968 and the humiliation and removal of Dubcek as First Secretary the following year saw the end to this brief period of artistic energy. Censorship was reimposed in 1969; by 1971 the Writers' Union was outlawed, the works of over eighty Czech writers had been banned and forty per cent of all Czech journalists had lost their positions. To humiliate them, they were offered menial jobs in order to earn a living. Experimental writing, or writing critical of the government, circulated privately as samizdat or underground publications and some of these found their way to the West where Czechoslovak émigrés helped to publish them. Nearly two decades would pass before the hidden networks which kept the artistic community alive could surface once more.

Edith's last two translations, both by major Czech writers, were published in 1970. *Mozart in Prague* was by Jaroslav Seifert, Chairman of the Writers' Union, who refused to support the new government under Party Chief Husak, saying to him, 'You want us to support your policies because you know that we enjoy moral authority in the nation. But should we support you, we would lose this authority and in such a case we would be of no use to you.' (Ulc p. 88) Seifert's book was published in Prague, but Ivan Klima's two political allegories published under the title *A Ship Named Hope* were only published in London. This was hardly surprising considering that 'A Ship Named Hope' is a fable about passengers on a doomed ship going on its last voyage, and the second story, 'The Jury', is a Kafkaesque tale about a prisoner in custody who curiously manages to guillotine himself while trying to escape.

With the Writers' Union banned and publishing effectively at a standstill, Edith felt that there was nothing further she could do: 'Everything in Prague was disrupted, half the staff of Artia, the foreign language publishing house, had escaped abroad or were suppressed, like all institutions that had shown liberal tendencies. There was simply no communication, and also nothing being published that one would consider translating. I had been doing commissioned translations only as a means to an end, in any case. The classics I wanted for myself I had already done, and I stopped giving time to translating in favour of my own work.' It was as though the early 1950s had returned and nothing could be done to help. Yet the haunting voice of the last hidden Czech radio station in Prague to continue broadcasting as the tanks rolled into Charles Square, calling out, 'Don't forget Czechoslovakia! Don't forget Czechoslovakia!', was a message to her and to many Westerners who felt that yet again Czechoslovakia had been betrayed.

Pargeter saw the situation as an example of weakness on the part of Russia, and although she felt that it was a tragedy, she was sufficiently philosphical to hope that there would soon be another opportunity for Czechoslovakia to regain its independence. In a pamphlet written for the British-Czechoslovak Friendship League later that year, on 28 October, 1968, Edith saluted fifty years of independence for the Czech nation. She wrote that 'of the sorrows of small nations there is nothing that you do not know, nothing you have not survived.' Yet in referring to the memorable year of 1968 she saw there:

> The example, never to be forgotten, of an inspired and unanimous national manifestation of heroism, the quiet, practical rare heroism whose true communal spirit was recognised by us all as something new under the sun. A heroism that drew the best from everyone, restored to those who had almost lost it their faith in man.

After the invasion, several of the writers that Pargeter knew left their country and became exiles in Europe and America. Edith's special friends, the friends made at that 1947 summer school, remained in Prague and eventually she had the satisfaction of seeing the gates open once more. Trips to Czechoslovakia became possible and her Czech friends were able to visit her in England at last.

In September 1993, having been to Hungary to see the filming of the first British television series of the Cadfael novels, Edith sat in a bookshop in Prague signing copies of *One Corpse Too Many* which had just been published in Czech. Hundreds of people queued up to meet her. Translations are continuing and there have been two adaptations of *Death and the Joyful Woman* for Czech television. Her enduring affection for the country has recently been recognised by the Prague Branch of the international writers' association P.E.N., who have made her an honorary member. She continues to be, in the words of Zora Wolfova, 'a great friend of our country, music and literature.'

Of the events in 1989 which finally brought political independence for the Czech and Slovak peoples, and set them free to travel and live as they would wish, Edith concluded her article for the Bulletin of the Welsh Academy by commenting:

> They and we have waited twenty-one years for what we knew must happen, since no empire lasts for ever. None of us expected it so soon or so suddenly and totally, the delayed Spring in full flower at last. I doubted if I should live to see it, but I have! Nunc dimittis!

'Pravda vitezi!' says the national device. 'Truth will prevail!'

4. Crime on the Borders:
The Felse Mysteries

It is the author who creates the crime
And picks the victim, this blonde dark girl sprawled
Across a bed, stabbed, strangled, poisoned, bashed
With a blunt instrument. Or the young middle-aged
Old scandalous and respected beardless greybeard
Destroyed most utterly by some unknown means
In a room with doors and windows 'hermetically sealed'.

So victims and means are found. As for the motive
It is often impersonal...
'The Guilty Party', Julian Symons

As with most practitioners of crime fiction, or 'mysteries' to use the American term, Ellis Peters has spent her energies in practising her craft rather than evolving theories about it. Her rare pronouncements on what lies behind her novels are therefore all the more interesting, and the most substantial is an essay called 'The Thriller is a Novel' in a collection called *Techniques of Novel Writing*, edited by E.S. Burack and published in Boston in 1973.

In this essay, Peters reveals the familiar irritation of mystery writers that they are not taken seriously by the literary establishment. This is in spite of respected authorities such as Professor Peter Cawelti of the University of Kentucky, who claims in his major critical volume *Adventure, Mystery and Romance* that 'the classical detective formula is perhaps the most effective fictional structure yet devised for creating the illusion of rational control over the mysteries of life' (p.137). In defending formula literature against charges that it is 'lowbrow', 'popular' and 'entertainment' Cawelti maintains that:

> The trouble with this sort of approach is that it tends to make us perceive and evaluate formula literature simply as an inferior or perverted form of something better, instead of seeing its 'escapist' characteristics as aspects of an artistic type with its own purposes and justification. After all, while most of us would condemn escapism as a total way of life, our capacity to use our imaginations to construct alternative worlds into which we can temporarily retreat is certainly a central human characteristic and seems, on the whole, a valuable one. (p.13)

Respected crime writers, too, have analysed the distinctive qualities of the genre: Julian Symons, H.R.F. Keating and P.D. James have all firmly seen the crime novel as defining the morality of the age. Yet even though P.D. James's *Devices and Desires* was short-listed for the prestigious Booker Prize in 1989, there was a great deal of literary sniping about the crime novel taking its place beside more 'serious' books.

In 'The Thriller is a Novel', Peters firmly states that the thriller must be taken seriously, even 'in a world where thrillers are hygienically segregated from so-called 'straight' novels, given to other reviewers, and allotted about one-twentieth the amount of review space.' (Twenty years later, the situation is basically unchanged.) As for many other crime fiction writers it is the handling of characterisation that holds the key to a successful work — 'a book about half-people is not for me' — says Peters. Yet pulling against this is always the demand of the mystery, the trap that the writer creates as soon as he or she follows this path and leaves the pure detective puzzle to successful practitioners such as Agatha Christie:

> The more truthfully and solidly you set each character up to view, three-dimensional, calculable (to the limited extent that any man is calculable), and open to sympathy, the better your readers will know him, and the more you are limiting your own field of action where the mystery is concerned. (p.216)

Inevitably Peters concludes that 'the genuinely perfect thriller — by my rules, of course! — has never yet been written, and possibly never will be.' But she sees this as a challenge that cannot be resisted:

> For the truth is that the thriller is a paradox. It must be a mystery. And it must be a novel. And it is virtually schizo-

phrenia to aim at both. But for the dedicated author nothing
less is conceivable. To lower your sights is unthinkable. You
might as well take to the modern 'straight' novel, currently
subsiding soggily into the morass of the non-novel. (p.214)

Julian Symons, writing on the crime novel in his classic book *Bloody
Murder* (1985), agrees. He feels that, 'the crime novelist is most often
a fictionally split personality. Half of him wants to write a novel
about people affected by crime, but the other half yearns to produce
a baffling mystery.'And although Symons is in accord with Peters
about the difficulties involved, he does not see it as being completely
impossible: 'When the fusion of puzzle and characterisation is perfect, as in *The Glass Key*, you have books produced in the form of
crime novels that have a claim to be considered as works of art.'
(p.164)

By the time Peters was writing 'The Thriller is a Novel' in 1973 she
was well experienced in the genre. After her apprentice crime novels
as Jolyon Carr and John Redfern in the late 1930s and early 1940s she
had concentrated on her war novels and her Czech experiences. She
returned to crime fiction in 1951 with the first of the Felse novels,
Fallen Into the Pit, which introduces George Felse, initially as Detective
Sergeant of the County CID based in the county town of Comerbourne, then, after promotion, as Detective Inspector. The thirteen
Felse novels go some way towards satisfying Peters' criteria about
blending the thriller and the novel. Great pains are taken to present
her detective as an ordinary man who gets tired and hungry and
short-tempered with his son. The atmosphere has a cosy 'family' feel
which wreathes the novels ultimately in a sense of warm security.
George's wife, Bunty, who gives up her career as a singer on
marrying a policeman, remains supportive, intuitive and comforting
throughout, while going a little grey. We see their only son Dominic
finish school and university and set off on various travels around the
world. Unusually for a childless woman, Peters often gives Dominic
and his friends a prominent role in the action, not always to the
advantage of her craft, as these novels can sometimes give the
impression of resembling not very credible children's adventure
stories. (*Holiday with Violence*, a non-Felse novel published in 1952,
falls into this category, despite its stylish use of Venice as a backdrop.)

Music and musicians play a great part in many of these books, even beyond the allusions to music that occur so frequently. Sometimes the music itself plays a substantive part in the plot, as in the case of the fujara and the modal folksong in *The Piper on the Mountain*, or the Mahler song which haunts the diva in *The House of Green Turf*, or the ballad of Gil Morrice in *Black is the Colour of My True-Love's Heart*. Love of music, and a considerable knowledge of it, she attributes to the early influence of her mother and the wide-ranging repertory she heard performed as a child. Given Edith's fondness for vocal music, it is hardly surprising that in establishing her characters for the first Felse novel, the detective's wife should be a singer.

The Felse novels seem to be most successful when they exploit the author's deep attachment to the border country that she knows so well. She has said that 'even in the modern suspense novels, which claim the privileges of imaginative fiction, Shropshire is very much a presence, on my mind and emerging from my mind, to colour and haunt the background in shadow while my characters move in the light of the foreground.' Shropshire became Midshire at an early stage in her writing, and the name is retained in the Felse novels: Shropshire — 'with its border ambivalence and western frontier of mysterious hills.' Comerbourne is the county town where the County Constabulary has its headquarters and its portrayal is lightly based on a number of small towns within reach of Shrewsbury, which is the real county town of Shropshire. Felse lives in an unremarkable house in the village of Comerford, ten minutes drive from his office. The village boasts the usual furnishings of a Midshire village: church, manor, pub, shop and primary school.

Fallen Into the Pit (1951) forms something of a transition between the wide-ranging themes of the war-time trilogy and the more restricted focus of the detective novel. This is the only Felse novel to be published as Edith Pargeter; all the others use the Ellis Peters pseudonym. It begins with the aftermath of war and feelings that are very similar to those expressed by Pargeter in her article for the *Sunday Chronicle*:

> The war ended, and the young men came home, and tried indignantly to fit themselves into old clothes and old habits which proved, on examination, to be both a little threadbare, and on trial to be both cripplingly small for bodies and minds mysteriously grown in absence. (p.1)

Conflict arises in Comerford through the presence of a young

German ex-prisoner-of-war who is working in the neighbourhood as a miner and seems deliberately to irritate wounds that have not yet healed. He terrorizes a Jewish woman who has married a local farmer, he insults a photograph of a miner's dead brother and in the ensuing knife fight he causes the local war hero to exercise great self-control in not killing him on the spot. When Helmut Schauffler is found murdered no one is sorry and, as nearly everyone has spoken ill of him at one time or another, Sergeant George Felse has a long list of suspects.

The guilt that the village inevitably shares is accentuated by the many war-time memories that the victim has stirred. Felse has had few murders to deal with in Comerford and sombrely realizes that 'murder is not merely an affair of one man killed and one man guilty; it affects the whole community of innocent people, sending shattering currents along the suddenly exposed nerves of a village; and the only cure for this nervous disorder is knowledge.' Suspicion spreads from house to house with the ex-commando Chad Wedderburn in the most vulnerable position. George Felse finds his role as policeman an uncomfortable one, since his sympathies lie with people he has known all his life and are now on his list of possible murderers.

The death of Schauffler leads several people in the village to confide to George their dissatisfaction with the England they returned to after the war — 'this damned inadequate society that's supposed to keep the rain off us.' There is a sympathetic portrayal of Gerd Hollins, the Jew who mistakenly hopes to overcome her past by befriending Schauffler. Murder starts to unravel the close ties of village life — 'for the crack in Helmut's head was also a crack in society, through which impulses from the outer darkness might come crowding in; and of disintegration all human creatures are mortally afraid.'

The author continues to explore the moral issues implicit in war and its aftermath, using Helmut as a focal point for the two extreme attitudes that she deplores: a too-easy desire to forgive German aggression, and on the other hand, the British habit of retreating into old attitudes that constrict aspirations towards a new society and stifle the desire to prevent future wars. As Chad Wedderburn explains to his scrapping schoolboys, physical conflicts 'always indicate a failure by *both* sides, wherever they occur.' And those who fought most bravely, like Chad and the quiet shepherd Jim Tugg, feel most strongly that the values they fought for must not be lost.

Jim is uncharacteristically eloquent when he bursts out to George, 'I wanted my war used properly. God damn it, didn't I have a right to expect it?'

With the solution of the murder, the threads of community life draw together once more and Comerford looks hopefully to the future. Like the open-cast mining surrounding the village, destructive forces can also sweep away old relics from the past and leave a new landscape to be shaped.

As a detective novel, *Fallen Into the Pit* suffers from the failure of Felse to develop as a strongly defined character directing events. His son, Dominic, is much more active and eventually implicates the murderer by deliberately putting himself in danger. The sense of place, of the small community with its particular landscape of abandoned industry co-exising with agriculture and the varied society that gathers nightly in 'The Shock of Hay' public house, evokes more response from the reader than the details leading to the solution of the crime. At the same time the well-developed supporting characters and the rich texture of the background provide a novel that is much more than a simple 'whodunnit', and Pargeter says that she had planned this more as a novel containing a murder than a murder novel. Subsequent books were to show how individual these border mysteries could be, using as major plot components a constant sensitivity to the landscape and a consciousness of the past.

Even though the Felse novels have a contemporary setting, an historical dimension is often at the heart of the mystery. In *Death and the Joyful Woman* (1961), for instance, an important strand in the plot is an old inn sign that ultimately turns out to be part of a medieval altar piece from Charnock Priory. Similar treasures feature in other novels, such as the illuminated manuscripts in *Rainbow's End* and the carved door in *The Knocker on Death's Door*. Pargeter placed these novels with precision:

> The landscape of these novels, nowhere exactly copying reality, follows the River Comer upstream from the county town of Comerbourne, in the plain, by way of the windings of the stream and the undulations of its accompanying road, up into the border valley of Middlehope, and over the watershed beyond the source of the river, to descend into Wales. Comerford, the first larger village in this upstream progression, is in process of being developed, and in danger of becoming a small town in the later novels, but is already in the uplands,

overhung to westward by the border hills. Further up the valley is Mottisham Abbey, the scene of *The Knocker on Death's Door*, and beyond that lies Abbot's Bale, invaded by incompatible strangers in *Rainbow's End*. With every mile up the valley the river grows smaller, the surroundings wilder, the farms more widely scattered, the names more Welsh, until the road crosses the watershed in bracken and heather and curlew's cries. The whole, though not copied accurately, would be recognised as the upper Teme Valley.

There is a timeless quality about this region, which strongly colours the atmosphere of *The Knocker on Death's Door*:

> Life did not change much in Middlehope. Why should it? The basic way of living here, in a hard but beautiful solitude, had been evolved long ago, and only minor adaptations had been made to them since. (p.4)

And there is little crime in the 'elusive world' of Middlehope, as George Felse's old friend Sergeant Jack Moon is well aware:

> 'Crime, by and large, we don't go in for. A bit of riotous behaviour now and again, that's about it. Sin, now, sin's more in our line.' The distinction was clear, thoughtful and comforting. (p.6)

Crimes in Middlehope often have a special quality that relates to outsiders attempting to change long-established practice. Wealthy antique dealer Arthur Rainbow makes a determined takeover bid for the village of Abbot's Bale in *Rainbow's End* (he even becomes church organist and throws out the familiar old tunes, replacing them with awkward modern pieces that no one one can sing) and ends up pushed from the church tower. Further crimes emerge from this, which relate to renovation work taking place in the ruins of Mottisham Priory, and bring in interesting aspects of late medieval church history.

The Knocker on Death's Door also sees an outsider summarily dispatched, this time a photographer from Birmingham who takes too much interest in the carved oak door on the local church. An intriguing mystery is gradually prised out of the fabric of the village and involves the local gentry, the Macsen-Martels, of Norman descent, who are responsible for a modern body inconveniently buried beneath the flagstones of their historic home, Mottisham Abbey. What characterises all police investigation in Middlehope is the close defensiveness of its residents against the outside world — 'one assault from an intruder, and the whole valley would clam up and present a united front of impenetrable ignorance, solid as a Roman shield-wall, in defence of its own people and its immemorial sanctity.'

Death and the Joyful Woman (1961), which won Peters her Edgar Allan Poe Award from the Mystery Writers of America in 1962, is one of the most praised of the Felse novels. This time historical interest stems from an ancient building which has been turned into a public house. Dominic Felse is only fourteen at the opening of the novel when he becomes infatuated with a wealthy heiress to a brewery who, two years later, is arrested on a charge of murder. Dominic, convinced of her innocence, finds himself in a complicated situation when for the first time his closeness to a police investigation causes him serious personal problems. He is now sixteen and feels he knows his own mind. In order to help the heiress, Kitty, he gives her information that he heard from George and Bunty as they chatted casually in the house:

> Never in his life before, not even as a small, nosy boy, had he betrayed a piece of information he possessed purely by virtue of being George's son. If he did it he was destroying something which had been a mainspring of his life, and the future that opened before him without it was lonely and frightening, involved enormous readjustments in his most intimate relationships, and self-searchings from which he instinctively shrank. But already he was committed, and he would not have turned back even if he could. (p.122)

Much of the novel's unique quality comes from the adolescent responses of Dominic and the puzzlement of his parents about his activities, which culminate in offering himself as bait to the real murderer. As well as exploring the white-water currents of young adults and their relationships, Peters provides a full cast of interesting characters. Several have motives for the spectacular killing of Alfred Armiger, including Leslie, his son, and there are many intricate plot strands to thicken the narrative. The Felse novels are most successful when the crime seems to grow up from local knowledge as it does here, rather than the transplanted tales which tend to show up the unconvincing edges in the portrayal of Dominic and his friends.

Flight of a Witch (1964) also has its historical references, but this time more ancient and less easily defined. The landscape of the novel is dominated by the Hallowmount, a mysterious hill on the border of Wales. Backed by the mist-wreathed mountains of the Welsh borders, the Hallowmount is crested by a ring of stunted trees and a rock called the Altar, and holds associations with witchcraft, Druids and ancient Christianity. When the school-master Tom Kenyon, a Londoner, sees the mountain for the first time he senses 'something of shadow and age and silence like a coolness cutting him off from the sun, not unpleasantly, not threateningly, rather as if he was naturally excluded from what embraced all other creatures here. He was the alien, not resented, not menaced, simply not belonging.' The Hallowmount is known to cast spells and to draw people into its power, although young Annet Beck exploits the mythology for her own purposes.

Detective Inspector Felse is again upstaged by the landscape and although ostensibly investigating a murder in Birmingham in which Annet may be involved, the activities surrounding the Hallowmount are much more engrossing. The mystery ends, appropriately enough, within the hollow at the crest of the hill, the site of many unknown pagan rites. By now Tom Kenyon feels less alienated from this cold and empty countryside, and as he keeps watch for young Annet and the probable murderer he begins both to accept the weight of centuries and to feel strangely at ease:

> He had no sense of undergoing a new experience; this was rather a recollection, drawn from so deep within him that he felt no desire to explore its origins, for that would have been dissecting his own identity, or to question its validity, for that would have been to doubt his own. He felt the tension of long ages of human habitation drawing him into the ground, absorbing him, making him part of the same continuity. (p.321)

Peters uses the Hallowmount, which is an amalgam of several mountains in the region, as the focal point of a murder mystery, yet the murder is no more than a functional plot device. The novel's fascination comes from her evocation of an ancient landscape and its interaction with contemporary society. Here, even Tom Kenyon's sixth-formers talk easily about the powers of the Hallowmount and 'found nothing incongruous in having one foot in the twentieth century and one in the roots of time', a situation one can only conclude seems entirely appropriate to this author.

The Felse family are on holiday in *A Nice Derangement of Epitaphs* (1965) but crime-solving follows them to a comfortable hotel on the north Cornwall coast. Again the focus is very much on the young people involved in unravelling the mystery and the effect on the innocent of buried truths unexpectedly brought to the surface. In this case they are literally exhumed, because most of the puzzle revolves around the opening of an eighteenth century family tomb and the deciphering of some cryptic epitaphs. The present is intertwined with the past as a recently drowned body is found where the remains of Jan Treverra should be.

Running parallel to the mystery in the tomb is a more modern, but equally complex network of emotions that surrounds an adopted child, Paddy Rossall. The security of Paddy's first fifteen years is about to be shattered by a determined bid by his real father to repossess him. Dominic Felse is now eighteen, with all the super-iority that this age brings, but he and Paddy still find enough in common to understand each other in a world that can often appear to be extremely fragile. Peters recognises that teenaged boys frequently feel awkward but despite her best efforts to deal with their difficulties her dialogue can be unintentionally uneasy, genuine though her sympathies are. The puzzle, however, is engrossing and full of fascinating twists and turns, with the eighteenth century story emerging as vividly as the conflicts in the present.

Human relationships rather than crime itself again continue to take centre stage in *Black is the Colour of My True-Love's Heart* (1967) and *The House of Green Turf* (1969). A very particular aspect of Shropshire landscape has its part to play in *Black is the Colour of My True-Love's Heart* which derives its setting from Attingham Park, near Shrewsbury, the venue for educational weekends for adults which Edith had worked to establish. Although Follymead in the novel is carefully described as a Gothic, not a neo-classical house, the flavour of a residential college, with its arbitrary assortment of young and old, is acutely observed. Peters still has a high regard for the college, and wrote in *Shropshire* that:

> Follymead's bizarre architecture bears no resemblance to Attingham's classic grandeur, nor are there any portraits among the students gathered for the occasion. But undoubtedly

the pleasure and the profit I derived from Attingham's memorable weekends, and the gratitude I felt for it, suggested the book, and it was written with affection. (p.164)

The exotic architecture of Follymead parallels the labyrinthine story which unfolds tragically during a weekend course on folk and ballad singing. The Warden of the College, Edward Arundale, quotes the Gothic novelist Horace Walpole, who supposedly stayed there, as saying that it was 'a house where drama was a permanent upper servant, eccentricity a member of the family, and tragedy an occasional guest.' And so it proves, with drama from the start when two famous singers clash violently, their love affair shattered by misapprehension and suspicion. The artificial park which surrounds the house, with its carefully designed vistas and engineered river banks — 'nature had abdicated, unable to keep up the pace' — reflects the apparently perfect marriage of the Arundales, 'the image of a successful, efficient, socially accomplished college head and his eminently suitable and satisfactory wife.'

As not one but two missing people need to be found, Detective Inspector Felse is quietly asked for his professional advice. Everyone is concerned for the good reputation of the college; the weekend course must continue and scandal be avoided. Thanks to a convenient suicide no charges need to be laid and the future of the college is unthreatened. Eighty satisfied students depart with their harps and guitars, their noisy background having provided an unknowing counterpoint to dramas as passionate as in any of their ancient ballads. Follymead is quiet at last, containing only two re-united lovers. As George Felse drives away he sees the house receding into the distance and becoming 'a harmonious, a symmetrical whole, making unity out of chaos.'

Bunty Felse stays very much in the background in most of the novels, but in *The Grass-Widow's Tale* (1968) she is at the centre of events. With Dominic away at university and George on a case in London she meets a young man in a pub and finds herself at the mercy of a murderous gang. As a thriller this novel is sharply focused and genuinely tense. What makes it unusual is the perceptive insight into the emotional state that a forty-one year old mum can find herself in, sitting solitary and alone on a rainy night, on the eve of her birthday. Bunty's crisis is not an unusual one and like many wives and mothers she wonders how her own life seems to have disappeared at the service of others:

> She felt time rushing away from under her feet, leaving her
> falling through space in a howling greyness. There had once
> been a certain Bunty Elliott who had known beyond question
> that she was going to be a great singer, and leave a treasury
> of recorded music that would make her immortal. But she had
> never put her gifts to any serious test, because she had met
> and married George Felse, and turned into a mere wife, a
> policeman's wife. And what was she now but George's wife
> — no, George's grass-widow at the moment, and this moment
> was her whole life in microcosm — and Dominic's mother?
> Did she exist, except as a reflection of them? Was she con-
> demned only to act, only to be anything at all through her
> husband and her son? (p.17)

Bunty becomes involved in unravelling the mystery because she
wants to feel needed according to her own merits, not because she
is a wife or mother. Although remaining unmarried herself, Peters
is remarkably understanding of Bunty's uncharacteristic state of
despair and this novel deepens her role substantially in the novels
which follow.

Psychological thrillers have never been Peters's special territory,
but *The House of Green Turf* (1969) reveals how successful she could
be in this genre. The novel begins with a traffic accident near Comerbourne where a beautiful young opera singer, Maggie Tressider, is
seriously injured. As she lies unconscious she becomes aware of an
accusing voice, a voice which continues to haunt her even when she
is recovering in hospital. Maggie calls in a private detective, not a
psychiatrist, to delve into her past and to try to find the incident
which leads to her overpowering sense of guilt at having somehow
caused the death of another person. Unpicking the past leads to a
European concert tour thirteen years before when Maggie was only
eighteen; curiously enough the person managing the tour was Ber-
narda Elliot, better known to readers as George Felse's wife, Bunty.
Most of the events in the novel take place in the Austrian Voralberg,
near Lake Constance, where Maggie was led to believe that a young
cellist drowned himself after being rejected by her. Bunty and
George follow the trail to Austria, where eventually an international
smuggling ring is uncovered, not entirely plausibly, and various
missing persons are accounted for. Maggie and her private eye keep

their distance while fighting their growing attraction, and eventually this successful but lonely woman, with a little help from Bunty and George, realises that she can find a space in her life for someone she can trust and admire as well as love.

In three of the later Felse novels, Peters seemed happy to move away from Shropshire but to use Dominic as her link to Midshire and George and Bunty at home. *The Piper on the Mountain* (1966) brings in Peters's latent affection for Czechoslovakia, and she takes the radical step of setting a crime novel there. Dominic Felse is now a first year university student, rattling round Europe with some friends in a third-hand VW van. None of the group realise that they are being carefully directed towards a particular destination by Tossa Barber, a member of the party whose stepfather Herbert Terrell had apparently suffered a fatal accident in the Tatra Mountains. Dominic has his father's observant eye and quickly becomes aware that a conspiracy is likely to engulf his headstrong friend. Peters revels in her descriptions of the high peaks of the Tatras and the brilliant, volatile skies. She lovingly tells us of the lace caps and embroidered skirts of the women and the swaggering cloaks and breeches of the shepherds. Her fondness for music also emerges with some esoteric information about the Slovakian pipes, including the great fujara which the fugitive plays so hauntingly.

Eventually the mystery unfolds and the trail leads back to England and Sir Broughton Phelps, an impeccable civil servant on close terms with the Minister. Had Peters been John le Carré there would have been rather more sardonic pleasure in exposing well-concealed corruption at the highest levels of British society. As it is, she explains but does not comment, leaving the expertise, and the moral high ground, firmly in Czechoslovakia, where the avuncular Lieutenant Ondrejov — 'more devious than his buccolic appearance suggested' — takes great pleasure in manipulating events to bring about the exposure of the murderer. He invites the British Consulate to sort out their own problems: '"England is your own house, gentlemen," said Ondrejov, "Set it in order yourselves."'

Professional writers often find that they can set novels in exotic landscapes very competently without ever having visited the location themselves. H.R.F. Keating wrote several novels featuring Inspector Ghote in Bombay before eventually making the trip to India. Ellis Peters's two Indian novels do have a three-month visit to India as a basis, when in 1961 she accepted an invitation to stay with diplomats that she had met in Prague. Midshire goes to India a few years later in the presence of Dominic Felse as amateur sleuth. *Mourning Raga* (1969) and *Death to the Landlords!* (1972) both feature young people as the crime-solving force but without the solid foundation of English country life to underpin them these novels lack solidity, no matter how hard Peters tries to infiltrate detailed descriptions of the streets of Delhi, Indian film crews and sitar music.

In *Mourning Raga*, Dominic and his girlfriend Tossa are asked to accompany fourteen-year-old Anjali, daughter of a film star and an Indian scientist, to visit her father in Delhi. Her kidnap and ransom, the murder of an old watchman and a chase through the streets of the city strain credulity and the events seldom rise near to the level that shows Peters at her best. Moral virtue is so overwhelming in the shape of a Swami who is also an agriculturalist and a wealthy father who intends to give everything to the poor that any concern about the endangered characters is minimal. As in the other Indian novel there is no real sense that the forces of evil could even begin to carry the day.

Death to the Landlords! (1972) is less conventional than the earlier novel and could have explored some interesting territory if given the chance to roam. Ruth Prawer Jhabvala has written several fine pieces of fiction about Anglo-Saxon women who fall under the power of religious and political groups in India and the potential exists in Peters's novel to write very revealingly on this theme. In creating Patti Galloway, who carries bombs for an extreme left-wing terrorist group dedicated to assassinating wealthy landlords, Ellis Peters has the opportunity to go some way towards explaining the role of the middle-class terrorist in the 1970s. Only when Patti has been blown up and killed by her own bomb does Dominic Felse begin to see the truth about his travelling companion:

> She came from England, already in rebellion against everything that represented her parents and the establishment. She came innocent, romantic, idealistic, silly if you like, a sucker for left-wing causes, and kidded into hoping to find the wonderful, easy, metaphysical way here in India. And India kicked her in the teeth, the way it does — in the belly, too, sometimes — showing her, as it shows to all silly idealists, its most deprived and venomous and ugly and venal side. She was absolutely ripe to be a fall guy. (p.496)

In *Death to the Landlords!* the positive, perhaps too virtuous characters include a wealthy landowner who is planning to give away his property and Priya, a young nurse, who takes on the role of the new Indian woman; competent, sensitive to tradition but not hidebound by constricting values. Dominic carries out his accustomed role of keen observer, accurate reporter and supporter of law and order yet his presence is shadowy in this novel and the author's interests seem much more drawn to the tensions in Indian society which she finds in the extreme left (represented by the terrorists) and the enlightened left (represented by the landowner). She also touches briefly on the predicament of the Indian returned from Europe and now feeling alienated from his own culture — 'he is homeless who has two homes' — is one of the author's favourite sayings. Unfortunately the conclusion of the novel leaves one feeling that the pressures of the thriller have again deflected attention from serious and interesting issues; a sense of superficial tidying up rather than a satisfying ambiguity at the end.

It is not surprising that having written three Felse novels set away from England, a return to Comerford would seem restricting. Only two more, *City of Gold and Shadows* (1973) and *Rainbow's End* (1978), were written. *City of Gold and Shadows* again shows Peters's imaginative approach to historical features in her own immediate surroundings. The Roman city of Viriconium (shown on contemporary maps as Wroxeter), about five miles south-east of Shrewsbury, is now bordered by a busy road where hundreds of cars and lorries race past daily. The ruins are extensive and indicate that this was England's fourth largest Roman city, with large public baths and the remains of a forum. Built originally as a 'rest and recreation' station for soldiers on the frontier — 'a pleasure city, quite unreal like all its kind' — Viroconium grew into a mixed settlement and thrived until Welsh raiders descended in the sixth century, and the settlement moved to the security of the loop in the river that became the city of Shrewsbury. The river Severn curves around the site, providing a necessary plot device, as the powerful flooding river breaks into the ruins, exposing new brickwork and threatening also to expose crimes that have up to now lain concealed. Peters uses the name *Aurae Phiala* for the ruined city in her novel, describing it in *Shropshire* as a projection, though not a portrait of Viriconium, and was certainly suggested by that haunting and haunted city.' (p.161) Peters gives the site a considerable degree of undefined menace:

A glass bowl of fragile relics closed with a pewter lid; and
outside, the fires of ruin, like a momentary recollection of the
night, how many centuries ago, when the Welsh tribesmen
massed, raided, killed and burned, writing 'Finis' to the history of this haunted city. (p.31)

The ghost of a Roman sentry, massive and helmeted, supposedly
walks the walls but in fact turns out to be a more substantial threat
to those who are trying to investigate a steady flow of Roman
artefacts on to the art markets of Europe. Peters achieves a narrative
tour de force in describing the struggle of the undercover policeman
Gus Hambro to escape from the underground hypocaust where he
has been thrown and expected to die. He crawls for over twenty
hours in the dark through the intersecting paths of the flues beneath
the hot room of the baths, encountering rats and a dead body on his
painful progress, until finally managing to break through where the
river has caused the land to slip away. Although human agencies
have their own responsibilities for murder and attempted murder at
Aurae Phiala, it is the river which, independent of human inter-
ference, directs the course of the action.

The Felse series is a valiant attempt to achieve what Peters, writing
about her craft in *Crime and Mystery Writers*, saw as 'the paradoxical
puzzle, the impossible struggle to create a cast of genuine, rounded,
knowable characters caught in conditions of stress, to let readers
know everything about them, feel with them, like or dislike them,
and still to try to preserve to the end the secret of which of these is a
murderer.'(p.848) Even so, murder is never an entirely negative force
in Ellis Peters since her novels often end with new relationships
established and lonely people finding suitable companionship.
Peters has seldom discussed the romantic element in her novels but
it is an important theme in every book and generally helps in the
feeling of reconciliation at the end. The landscape, too, is an inesca-
pable feature in these novels, which frequently juxtapose contemporary society with its visible and invisible past. History is seen not
only in its artefacts but as a hidden layer in society, often unexplored,
and revealing itself through earthworks, Roman roads, and ancient
graves. The river Severn, quiet and pastoral most of the time, is never
underestimated as a powerful and unpredictable force, bringing
flood waters from the Welsh mountains.

The main weakness of all the Felse novels is the character of George

Felse himself. Neither as a policeman nor as an individual does he acquire sufficient presence to be an entirely satisfactory creation, even though other characters respect and admire him. The routine of actual police work clearly fails to interest Peters and she provides the minimum detail possible. Forensic evidence does not feature heavily in these novels, nor does the teamwork involved in police investigations. All these aspects of everyday policing would have brought Felse in from the background where he often seems to be placed. But to focus more directly on Felse would be to deflect the reader's view from other characters, whose relationships, often with intricate and ingenious antecedents, prove to be very fascinating indeed.

Edith Pargeter's admission that the quality of 'good' is more interesting to her than the quality of 'evil' in her created characters reveals perhaps why her modern crime novels cannot be considered alongside works by such powerful contemporary writers as P.D. James and Ruth Rendell (who also writes as Barbara Vine). That, and a horror of violence for its own sake, make her work appeal to crime fiction readers who prefer to keep away from the uglier details of violent death and the psychopathology of killers.

P.D. James's series detective Adam Dalgleish is a subtle and sophisticated thinker who shares with the reader his comprehension of extreme emotional states and his realisation of the dangers that can lie beneath the most unlikely surfaces. In many of James's novels there is a genuine sense of evil and the resolution of the novel can bring to the reader a reward that is related to the menacing journey that has been undertaken. Similarly, Ruth Rendell's many disturbing studies of obsession go deep into the relationship between the criminal and the victim. Her focus is unrelenting and although some would argue that mental imbalance is less challenging in a crime than an exploration of the concept of evil, Rendell's characters are unforgettably portrayed. Even her Inspector Wexford novels, which are more straightforward in their plots than the psychological thrillers, have a robust connection with present-day problems and a genuine sense of the frustrations of home and family life.

Edith Pargeter's Inspector Felse novels have their own particular qualities and their border settings certainly give them an unusual texture. But had Pargeter not gone on to find a distinctive niche with the Brother Cadfael novels it is unlikely that the crime-writing side of her literary output would have been considered as more than a

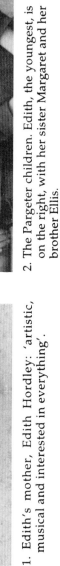

2. The Pargeter children. Edith, the youngest, is on the right, with her sister Margaret and her brother Ellis.

1. Edith's mother, Edith Hordley: 'artistic, musical and interested in everything'.

4. Edith's sister, Margaret, as a young woman.

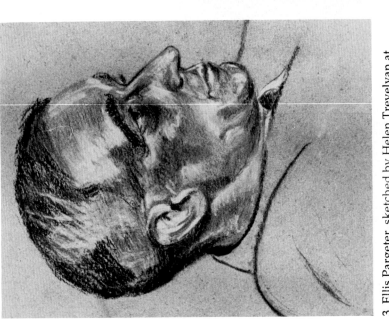

3. Ellis Pargeter, sketched by Helen Trevelyan at the WEA College, Attingham Hall.

5. Petty Officer Edith Pargeter was awarded the British Empire Medal in 1944 for her wartime service in the WRNS.

6. The Operations Room at Western Approaches Command Centre, Derby House, in Liverpool. Edith worked here as a teleprinter operator during World War Two. On these huge maps the Battle of the Atlantic was plotted and controlled.

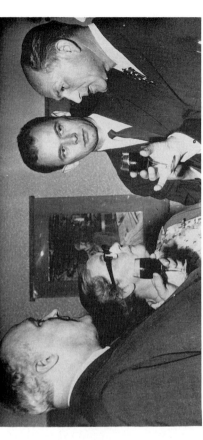

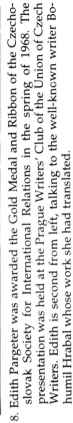

8. Edith Pargeter was awarded the Gold Medal and Ribbon of the Czecho-slovak Society for International Relations in the spring of 1968. The presentation was held at the Prague Writers' Club of the Union of Czech Writers. Edith is second from left, talking to the well-known writer Bohumil Hrabal whose work she had translated.

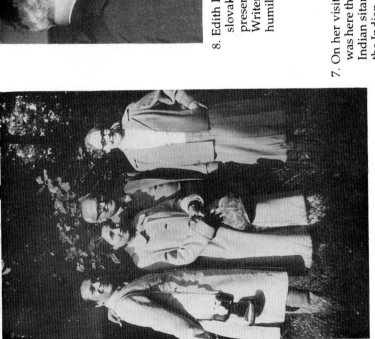

7. On her visits to Prague, Edith often met other international artists and it was here that she first met her Indian friends. Ravi Shankar, the celebrated Indian sitar player is on the left, with Edith on the right, standing beside the Indian Ambassador.

9. 'The Bard' was painted in 1817 by the visionary artist, John Martin. It reveals the fascination which Celtic history held for the nineteenth century romantic movement. In the painting the only Welsh bard to survive a massacre by Edward I pours curses on the seemingly endless forces of the English king. The castle is based on Harlech, although the scenery is highly romanticised.

10. Historical research is taken seriously, although Edith claims that it is always a pleasure. The small china bust in the background is her Edgar Allan Poe Award, given to her by the Mystery Writers of America.

11. Edith visits the set for the television productions of four of the Chronicles of Brother Cadfael. Shrewsbury Abbey was reconstructed near Budapest for the filming.

moderate success. By the mid 1970s Peters felt that she had reached the end of this particular creative seam, and wisely embarked on a new and very profitable vein of ore. Two novels, independent of any series, *The Horn of Roland* (1974), a love story set in Austria that is shadowed by an incident from World War II, and *Never Pick up Hitch-Hikers!* (1976), an adventure for young people set in a New Town remarkably like Telford, provided a standing point from which she could think about a new imaginary world, a world that was going to provide a perfect opportunity to draw together her unique feeling for history and her sharp sensitivity to the undercurrents that lead to crime.

But before considering the sources that led to the Chronicles of Brother Cadfael, it is essential to appreciate that other forms of fiction were also emerging in the late 1950s and 1960s. As well as the Czech translations, Pargeter continued to write short stories on a regular basis. She has always felt that the short story was not her metier and has said in her interview with June E. Prance that:

> I'm not terribly good at short stories. I've written quite a few
> but I find them more difficult. I need the elbow room of the
> novel. I need space for descriptions and for dallying with
> things like the weather, and for people to contemplate. That's
> hard to do in short stories. (p.16)

Nevertheless she has, over the years, written many short stories, most of which remain uncollected after publication in such magazines as *Argosy, Good Housekeeping, Everywoman, This Week, Woman and Home, Modern Woman, Reveille* and *Ellery Queen's Mystery Magazine*. These stories explore a wide variety of incidents and only some deal with crime. As the reader would expect, her short stories are well-crafted and perceptive; often throwing an unexpected light on human relationships.

Her three collections represent the range of her short fiction and also show how it relates to the longer works that were engaging her interest at the time. *The Assize of the Dying*, published as an Edith Pargeter title by Heinemann in 1958, contains three long stories, each with a romantic element. 'The Assize of the Dying' is almost novella length and is based on a dramatic fourteenth century Spanish tale. A man wrongly accused of murder and executed summons the Judge, the Foreman of the Jury, the Counsel for the Prosecution and the murderer to meet him in the Assize of the Dying. Very soon all have met violent deaths. 'Aunt Helen' reveals an interesting psychological approach to murder when a possessive woman, thought to be perfect by everyone, is unable to cope with the idea of losing her husband to someone else. 'The Seven Days of Monte Cervio' uses the time-honoured formula of skiers trapped in a high mountain hut after an avalanche who realise that they are in the presence of a murderer.

The second collection, *The Lily Hand and Other Stories*, published in 1965, again as Pargeter, contains fourteen stories all very different in tone. Some are warmly humorous, like the saga of the Town Band in 'Trump of Doom'; some explore unusual situations as in 'All Souls' Day' which looks sympathetically at the fate of refugees in an English camp after the War who are torn between common sense, which tells them to take advantage of the opportunity to make a new life in America, and their emotional longing to return to their home in Czechoslovakia. 'My Friend the Enemy' is a passionate monologue about the nature of war and like 'The Purple Children' takes the reader to conflicts overseas. This collection demonstrates the breadth of vision that has always characterised Pargeter's work.

She published the third collection, *A Rare Benedictine*, as Ellis Peters with Headline in 1988. Three longish stories all deal with Brother Cadfael but the first is certainly the most interesting because, eleven years after the first chronicle, *A Morbid Taste for Bones*, the author fills in some biographical details about her protagonist. She explains that the desire for continuity in her novels persuaded her not to go back in time to Cadfael's adventures in the Crusades even though many readers may feel that there are some stirring adventures waiting to be brought to life. A short story, standing on its own, gave Peters a welcome opportunity 'to shed light on his vocation.' 'A Light on the Road to Woodstock', with the biblical echoes of its title, summarises many aspects of Cadfael's character that have already emerged gradually in the preceding novels. Peters's comparison between Cadfael's conversion to the religious life and the actions of the sannyasi in India who put by worldly goods and set out with nothing but a begging bowl to gain merit in heaven reveals that she sees Cadfael very much as a force for good in the world. The other two stories in the collection, 'The Price of Light' and 'Eye Witness', deal efficiently with the standard ingredients of the Cadfael world and could both easily form part of a more extensive narrative.

These collections of short stories may lack the rewarding detail of the novels, yet they are far from negligible achievements. For a born storyteller such as Pargeter, it is almost impossible to produce a tale that does not hold the reader. Her ability to draw her public into an entirely alien world and to sustain this fictional control is best seen in the extensive historical sagas that were running parallel to the Felse fiction, the historical novels based on the struggles for control along the restless border between England and Wales from the thirteenth to the fifteenth century.

5. A Turbulent History

I am spellbound in a place of spells. Cloud
changes gold to stone as their circled bones
dissolve in risen corn.
                              'At Ystrad Fflur', Gillian Clarke

Long live the Prince of Wales!' This orchestrated cry greeted
Prince Charles, descendent of a titled German family, who
claimed his rights to the Principality in 1969. The significance of his
title and the echoes of that proclamation can be traced back through
time to the earliest stirrings of Welsh nationality. The title Prince of
Wales was fought for and won in the thirteenth century by Prince
Llywelyn of Gwynedd (1229-1282), having gained the support of
rival princes and for a short time having brought them to speak with
one voice against the English monarchy. Llywelyn's claim was recognised first in June 1265 after he had joined forces with Simon de
Montfort to defeat the forces of Henry III at the Battle of Lewes. Two
years later the Treaty of Montgomery, made with a resurgent Henry,
confirmed the title. The Welsh were to retain it only until Llywelyn's
death in a skirmish with the soldiers of Edward I near Builth, on 11
December 1282. Edward then gave the title to his son, Edward II, and
with it went all hopes of nationhood. As John Davies notes of the
passing of Llywelyn in his *History of Wales*:

> With his death, the keystone was destroyed and the Welsh
> polity which he and his ancestors had fostered was uprooted,
> a polity which, as yet, has had no successor. Henceforth, the
> fate of the Welsh in every part of their country would be to
> live under a political system in which they and their charac-
> teristics would have only a subordinate role, a fact which
> would be a central element in their experience until this very
> day and hour. (p.161)

In drawing the link between past and present Professor Davies makes an important point about Wales, and for any country that has had to establish and defend a borderline. Consideration of the past is crucial to a contemporary identity and our postmodern longings may account, to some extent, for the current popularity of historical fiction.

Historical novels have, for many years, been marginalised by the literary world just as crime fiction has been. Once categorised as producers of 'popular fiction', such writers as Mary Stewart, Georgette Heyer and Catherine Cookson have never been taken seriously, despite their enormous readerships. Recently, however, the creative possibilities that open up through the filtering of time have begun to appeal to other novelists. William Golding's *Rites of Passage* (1980), Peter Ackroyd's *Hawksmoor* (1985), Barry Unsworth's *Sacred Hunger* (1992) and Thomas Keneally's *The Playmaker* (1987) have all been highly esteemed. These novels function because there is a constant and revealing interplay between the contemporary reader and the historic past. As Australian novelist Patrick White observed in his self-portrait *Flaws in the Glass* (1981) with regard to readers of his historical novel *A Fringe of Leaves*, 'they sense in its images and narrative the reasons why we have become what we are today.'

For Edith Pargeter the past has always been a touchstone for the present. Her ability to recreate the living sense of a world beyond her own was well established in her Second World War trilogy, *The Eighth Champion of Christendom*. Then, in the late 1950s, as she was writing the early Felse novels and other popular fiction, her acute sense of the past led her to begin writing a series of novels based on the history of the borders. She was creating with an imaginary world of eight hundred years ago, yet traces of this world could still be discovered around her as she wrote. In her recent book *Shropshire* Pargeter describes how the atmosphere of the novels evolved from their setting:

> *The Heaven Tree* and its sequels took me over a good part of western Shropshire in a roving refresher course, especially along the Roman road on the flank of the Long Mountain, with the Breiddens looming at the northern end of the ridge, and a grand, stormy view of the river valley, the meadows that hold all that remains of Strata Marcella, and the town of Welshpool. This was still history, even though the fictional story woven into it took pride of place, so all that was historical had to be

exact. But the castle that never existed I could place where I chose, provided I took care to account for its absence in the end.

This is my favourite of all my work, the one that comes nearest to what I wanted it to be. (p.160)

But historical facts, as always with Pargeter, are paramount: 'when writing history, even in the form of fiction, every documented and ascertainable fact must be respected, and an effort made to present events and locations as truly as possible.'

During the twelfth and thirteenth centuries the border between England and Wales was characterised by uncertainty, tension and sometimes brutal conflict. The powerful and independent Marcher Lords, secure in strongholds along the Border, held the balance between the Welsh princes and the King. Within the main territory of Wales there was acute rivalry between the princes. They made and broke alliances easily and were regarded as barbarians by much of Europe. Henry II wrote to the Byzantine emperor that 'The Welsh are a wild people who cannot be tamed.' Even the establishment of religious houses in Wales (mainly Benedictine and Cistercian) in the twelfth century served to consolidate Welsh language and culture rather than to imprint Norman forms. By establishing a prosperous wool trade the monasteries flourished, but they looked to the charismatic Welsh princes who had founded them for protection, not to Canterbury or Rome. In 1159 the Archbishop of Canterbury wrote to the Pope that 'the Welsh are Christian in name only', and King John, some years later, threatened to pull down the monastery of Strata Florida because 'it harboured our enemies.'

John became King of England in 1199 and his seventeen-year reign lies behind the first volume of *The Heaven Tree* trilogy. It was a restless period that culminated in the sixty-three clauses of Magna Carta which the Barons forced John to sign in 1215. A year later John was dead, and his nine-year old son, Henry III, was crowned as his successor. Henry was fortunate in his protectors and only when he reached the age of majority did the stability of the kingdom seriously waver. His judgements were erratic and he was a poor judge of men. Dante placed him in the part of Purgatory reserved for simpletons and children. During his reign he made an attempt to curb the power of the Marcher Lords and, not surprisingly, they resisted strongly. A famous story tells of a hapless royal messenger delivering a summons to Walter de Clifford, Lord of Llandovery, and being made to eat the whole parchment, not forgetting the seal. Within Wales, Llywelyn the Great (1172-1240) had grown in power and had begun to refer to himself as Prince of Wales, an important stage in establishing the Principality as an independent nation. His grandson Llywelyn's status as Prince of Wales was recognised by Henry III in the terms of the Treaty of Montgomery in 1267, providing, in the words of Professor John Davies, 'proof that there were in medieval Wales all the elements necessary for the growth of statehood.'

The Heaven Tree Trilogy, comprising *The Heaven Tree* (1960), *The Green Branch* (1962) and *The Scarlet Seed* (1963) takes place against this background of growing Welsh nationalism and tension between the borders and the throne. The three novels are closely linked together and cover about thirty-five years in time, from 1200 to 1234. In Wales power is growing in the hands of Llywelyn ap Iorwerth, of Gwynedd, later known as Llywelyn the Great. The central character, Harry Talvace, is a younger son in a family descended from proud Norman stock. His studies at Shrewsbury Abbey, in the company of his foster-brother, the stonemason's son Adam Boteler, have included the ability to carve in stone in the Abbey yard; not an attribute considered worthy of a descendent of the family of the Earl of Shrewsbury. More seriously, Harry is an independent thinker who sees clearly the social injustices surrounding him. His position requires him to defend a system of feudal law that he cannot, morally, support. His early rebellion against his family is repeated many times throughout his life as he defends the helpless and attacks injustice. Harry remains a dynamic and fascinating character until his early death at the hands of Ralf Isambard, Lord of the castle of Parfois, which he has raised high on a rocky outcrop on the Welsh borders. Isambard and Parfois are imaginary creations; the power of a Marcher Lord is not.

Harry Talvace's greatest achievement as a stonemason is the building of a church for Parfois; in it he realises all his skill and his artistic vision. But his pledge to complete the church and his acute sense of honour and justice lead inevitably to a conflict with Isambard. Harry completes the church in chains and as he is led to execution he sees the perfection of his creation:

> He halted, looking up from the shadowy ground, up the delicate tapering lines of the buttresses, up the loftly sweep of

the wall, to the tower. The light from the east touched the cool grey stone and it blazed into gold. Every pinnacle was an ascending flame. Stage upon stage, the tower drew upwards its gleaming walls, its taut, true, pure brush-strokes of light and shadow, until the golden stem burst into the pale, shining flower of the sky.

He stood with uplifted face, dazzled with delight, worshipping the work of his hands. (p.333)

The Heaven Tree ends on a note of considerable drama as Harry's wife and newly-born son flee from Isambard's rage in the company of his mistress, Madonna Benedetta. They ride in desperation to Prince Llywelyn the Great, who has just captured the town of Shrewsbury, and throw themselves on his mercy.

In writing *The Heaven Tree*, Pargeter was conscious that she was celebrating a magnificent period of English art and she tells us in *Shropshire* that:

It is the period and the style I wanted to use as the peak of a great art, and in this manifestation hardly found out of England, in *The Heaven Tree*. That book was conceived not necessarily as an historical novel, but as an attempt to create a credible artist, even a great artist, and to set him in his own society, whatever the period; and whatever the period, I was certain he would find himself to some extent in collision with society, by virtue of the very qualities of proportion and balance that made him an artist. For someone else it could have been set in another period, even this one. For me it began in 1200 or so simply because I regarded the building of the great cathedrals as about the highest achievement of human talent and skill, a peak in art, and the particular excitement of the stiff-leaf carving, its sheer organic energy, truth and power, seemed to me a peak upon a peak. So the time was laid down for me. (p.95)

In *The Green Branch*, the second volume of the trilogy, Harry Talvace's son, also named Harry, grows up to be as unruly as his father. He is raised as a Welshman in the court of the Prince of Gwynedd, but he also knows that he is English. The lovely Madonna Benedetta, with her glorious red hair, has become an anchorite, in the old Celtic tradition, living beside St Clydog's cell in the uplands above the prince's palace at Aber. In *The Green Branch* the battle between Isambard and young Harry begins; a battle that first shows

Harry as desperate for revenge for his father's death, and ends, in *The Scarlet Seed*, with hatred turning into a fierce respect, if not love, for his enemy.

Harry recklessly climbs the steep cliff into the lofty castle of Parfois and is held prisoner after vainly attempting to kill Isambard in his father's church. Isambard sardonically regards him as a worthy opponent, telling him, 'Save all that fine, lusty hatred for me. I am the only enemy here worth your steel.' From now on the narrative charts the tension between them as Harry remains as a prisoner in Parfois and his friends are helpless to rescue him. He is released briefly to assist Llywelyn in battle but knows that his sense of honour requires him to go back to captivity:

> I am the keeper of more than my own honour. He wills to break me, to find the weaknesses in me and prise me apart. And could he do it, he would have ruined more than me. My father had the better of him at all points, him he never could move. Could he bring me to break faith, or to fall short by the least grain of what I owe, I think he would be eased of something that poisons and darkens his life. And I would rather die than give him that satisfaction. (p.274)

The final volume of the trilogy, *The Scarlet Seed*, begins in 1232, the year when the justiciar of England, Hubert de Burgh, Earl of Kent, opposes the King's grandiose plans to invade France, which he sees as wasting English blood and English money. News of his dismissal and humiliation swept through the kingdom. Many barons defended him because de Burgh had maintained England for its lords, in opposition to the French opportunists who flowed into Henry's court seeking honours and lands. (This story is developed in a further novel, *The Marriage of Meggotta*, written in 1979.) Ralf Isambard, the fictional Marcher Lord, is a supporter of de Burgh, and in a brilliantly dramatised scene he confronts the King in Shrewsbury Abbey:

> King Henry held audience before supper in the great guest chamber of Shrewsbury Abbey, in a gilded chair set up on a dais draped with gold and red brocades and velvets, and against a backdrop of tapestries unrolled not two hours earlier from the pack-saddles of his unwieldy train. He was in high spirits, and even for him inordinately fine, with jewels in his

ears and on his long, fastidious fingers. The nobility of the march bruised their loyal lips on his gold-set rubies, and trod delicately about the skirts of his glittering gown. The air still quivered faintly with the reverberations of a resounding fall; they breathed the dust from it, and held their breath. He felt the tension of awe that held them poised against him, and a sweet excitement filled him. (p.38)

Isambard taunts and challenges the young King and stalks haughtily from the chamber after having been dismissed, his richly-clad knights closing around him. The scene is vividly etched and full of menace, the language perfectly reflecting the struggles of men on whose orders death and destruction lie readily in wait. For Isambard, his insolence and defiance are part of a pleasurable game:

The king heard them go, and shook with an anguish of detestation. How dared they, how dared they withdraw from his censure with the discipline and assurance of conquerors? How dared that man, that gilded memento mori, gather up the honours from between them with a sweep of his bony hand, and leave his lord here bereft and disparaged?

Isambard rode easily, the reins loose over his wrist, the smile still touching his mouth. They were out of sight of the wall of Shrewsbury, and pacing the broad grassy verge of the Roman road, when he suddenly put back his iron-grey head and laughed aloud. All this for de Burgh!

'God's wounds!' said Isambard to the green dusk that hung like a silver-sewn web over his head. 'You would think I loved the man!' (pp.48-49)

The saga culminates with the destruction of the castle and church of Parfois by Llywelyn's army as they return north after sacking Builth and Brecon. The old lord is now blind and his son William, who is even more ruthless than his father, has come to claim his inheritance. Also drawn back to the helpless Isambard, after many years, is Madonna Benedetta. Harry knows that his ancient enemy is about to be defeated as he has wished for so long. Yet his hatred has gradually disappeared. He tries to explain his feelings to a puzzled Llywelyn, who begins to understand what has happened to Harry's desire for revenge:

Man proposes, man performs; but God turns the very ground on which he stands, and leads him to a consummation he

never foresaw. He rides to destroy his enemy, and arrives to
deliver him. Well, so be it. God knows what he is about. (p.200)

What Harry can never forgive is Isambard having plundered his
father's grave as a final blow to the man he had killed. Only at the
end, when the church is ablaze and the proud castle is shaking on its
foundations, does Harry discover that several years before Isambard
had brought his father to lie beneath the altar of his great creation,
the church of Parfois.

As the castle and the church gradually disintegrate around the
bodies of Isambard, Benedetta and Talvace, the dressed and carved
stone is quietly pillaged and takes new form in the houses and
villages round about. Talvace's wonderful, almost vain-glorious
creation, born of pride and completed in anger, is reduced to a ruin.
Young Harry overcomes his desolation at the sight by finding that
the the glowing stone is now scattered through the landscape — 'that
communicable fire scattered now so widely' — and is bringing joy
to unexpected places. He turns his back on Parfois, and on England,
seeking his wife and his craft in Wales.

Pargeter's trilogy exemplifies many of the finest aspects of historical writing and creates a unique and impressive tapestry of border
history. The vision of Harry Talvace, artist and craftsman, and the
spiritual and moral growth of his son are brilliantly portrayed, as is
the icy attraction of Ralf Isambard. The fruits of Pargeter's wide
historical knowledge are expertly utilised as locations change, characters grow older and seasons pass. But her greatest achievements
are undoubtedly the creation of a border landscape painted on a
series of stunning canvases and the sustained use of an historical
vernacular language, which with very few exceptions, rings true
throughout the novels.

The Heaven Tree trilogy succeeds in novelistic terms because the
focus remains firmly on the imaginary characters Harry Talvace and
his son. Historic events may ebb and flow from the prince's palace
at Aber down the length of the Welsh border but the story of the
younger Harry and his growth in understanding as he matures takes
the foreground in the second and third novels. Pargeter is unable to
achieve this freedom from events in *A Bloody Field by Shrewsbury*
(1972) which is directed not by fictional characters but by actual
historical figures.

Pargeter admits to having had this book in her mind for ten years before she began to write it and she accumulated as much information as possible about the Battle of Shrewsbury in 1403 which forms the tragic climax to the novel. She writes in *Shropshire* that:

> I tried to describe the battle and the battlefield with strict precision, just as I tried to portray the three embattled Henrys as a great deal of reading and thinking had made me see them. I had that book in my mind, and indeed on my mind, for ten years before I began to write it. It was one of the most bitter and destructive clashes on English ground, and it happened in my own native county. I could not let it slip away without examining fully the circumstances that led up to it, and the consequences that followed it (p.160).

The battle, in which over four thousand men died, was fought on a plain three miles north-east of Shrewsbury. The site, now known as Battlefield, is marked by the beautiful church of St Mary Magdalen which Henry IV had constructed to commemorate the dead.

For most people, the Battle of Shrewsbury is inextricably bound up with Shakespeare's version of events in *Henry IV Part One*. While Shakespeare was brilliantly skilled in using his materials to produce great poetic drama, it was very far from historical fact. In the play Prince Hal and Hotspur are apparently equal in age and mettle, leading to a rousing exchange of chivalric challenges and a stirring duel on stage. The death of Hotspur is seen as the end of an era of romance and although Hal mourns him as an honourable opponent, not as a traitor, the audience is unfailingly led to see Hotspur, not Hal, as the hero of the hour.

The facts were considerably different. Hal was only a boy when the battle took place and Hotspur was older than Henry IV. Pargeter uses the age difference between Hotspur and Hal to point up the close bond between them, with Hotspur showing much more affection than Hal's own father, and to explain Hal's despair at Hotspur's humiliated corpse. The lyrical scene before the battle where Owain Glyn Dwr and Hotspur meet with their ladies and Owain's wife sings in Welsh is unlikely to have taken place, but its tone indicates that Shakespeare, too, found the Welsh romantic.

The fictional characters of Julian Parry and her father Rhodri, a Welsh wool merchant living in Shrewsbury, would normally represent the ordinary citizens of the town. But with Owain Glyn Dwr threatening the Borders, the Welsh are regarded as enemies and forbidden civil rights. Their house is sacked and Rhodri killed by townspeople lashing out at supposed traitors. Julian is one of Pargeter's brave and independent young women who has fallen under the charismatic spell cast by Henry Percy but she remains a marginal figure as events move relentlessly on towards his destruction. Although Percy loses the battle his noble qualities keep his memory alive. The king does not survive him by many years and dies in 1413, still filled with guilt at the deposition of Richard II.

Pargeter handles the affairs of state with confidence and the conferences of the leaders can often be subtly and revealingly portrayed. The horror of the battle itself is memorably described: 'flourishing fields trampled and harrowed and littered with dead and dying, cast weapons and bloodied armour and the rags of horses and men.' It must be admitted, however, that though Shakespeare's characters are historically inaccurate, their presence in the play is much more vivid than their presence in the novel. Yet even today Harry Hotspur's legacy is a powerful one and the history of the proud Percies of Northumberland can still be seen in the chain of castles that defends the coast from Warkworth to Berwick and along a shifting northern border which, like the Welsh, was to be many times bathed in blood before a lasting peace with the Scots was reached.

By the 1970s a combination of deep empathy with her subject and refined narrative skills allowed Pargeter to impose a clear pattern on one of the most chaotic periods of history. The four novels which make up *The Brothers of Gwynedd* quartet were published between 1974 and 1977, although their genesis goes back some considerable time. Pargeter regards these novels as being among the most important works that she has written, dealing as they do with historical events that are seldom noted outside Wales, and celebrating the life of a great Welsh leader. She has said that:

> I think the fictional biography of Llywelyn ap Griffith important because I went to great trouble to dig up every source and every detail I could find, and changed nothing of what I found. And because as far as I know no one, Welsh or English, has produced anything so complete about him before. The facts I uncovered determined my attitude. I found myself revering Llywelyn and loathing Edward. I even found it possible to make a case for David.

Events in the quartet range from Easter 1228, at the opening of

Sunrise in the West, to the death of Llywelyn the Great in 1240, then through the conflicts and triumphs depicted in *The Dragon at Noonday* and *The Hounds of Sunset* to the final defeat of the Welsh cause in 1282, and the death of Llywelyn, Prince of Wales, told in *Afterglow and Nightfall*. The chronicler at the heart of all four novels is Samson, illegitimate son of a waiting woman who grows up to become confidential clerk and secretary to Lord Llywelyn ap Griffith, who took the title Prince of Gwynnedd from his grandfather, Llywelyn the Great. Samson's loyalty to Llywelyn and to Wales is absolute. Like young Harry Talvace in *The Heaven Tree* trilogy he is a survivor when much of the proud nobility of Wales is destroyed. His pragmatic view of the changing fortunes of Llywelyn and his brothers and his selfless devotion to Cristin, a married woman whom he loves, provides a useful counterpoint to the rhetoric of the princes. Samson gives the administrator's eye to the detail of battle and the provisioning of castles. As a clerk he is free to mingle at all social levels and he proves useful to Llywelyn on many occasions as his eyes abroad. He travels to London and even to France to bring back Eleanor, daughter of Simon de Montfort, to be Princess of Wales. The personalisation of history comes about readily through this character, who is able to give the reader first-hand witness of the rise and fall of a great leader and his volatile brothers as well as the growing tyranny of Edward I towards Wales.

Prince Llywelyn is presented from the beginning as an heroic figure, a noble prince with all the virtues:

> There was an ordinary man's solemnity and dread in him, beholding as he did with wide-open eyes the immensity of the burden that lay upon him. And upon him alone, for there was no other being in all this land of Wales who could lift any part of that load from him. He knew it without pride, and accepted it without reluctance, but the weight of what he carried was a fearful and a wonderful thing. (p.328)

He is both statesman and warrior: tall, his hair burnished, his face, in Samson's words, like 'the rocks of Snowdon, and his eyes those silent lakes between.' The rebellion of Earl Simon de Montfort against the king is charted in all its hopes and final catastrophe. Earl Simon's daughter, Eleanor, becomes Princess of Wales having been imprisoned for several years by King Edward. Their life together is short but Llywelyn's great love for Eleanor helps him to bear the destruction of his kingdom. Throughout the saga the focal point is always with Llywelyn in Wales, not with the English. The moving descriptions of the Prince's death and the pitiless detail of the barbaric execution of his mercurial brother David at the High Cross in the centre of Shrewsbury bring the series to a powerful conclusion.

Pargeter's touch is more delicate in *The Marriage of Meggotta*, which was published in 1979, two years after the first Chronicle of Brother Cadfael. By this time Pargeter had steeped herself in historical research and was able to use it effortlessly in building up her characters. In telling the poignant story of Meggotta de Burgh and Richard de Clare the author develops real figures as freely as though they were imaginary, and does so with no loss in historical truth. She overcomes the slightly stilted respect for her subject that restrains the life of *A Bloody Field by Shrewsbury* and devotes her best sympathies to presenting a love story between children; not an easy task to achieve without becoming maudlin. The list of primary sources at the end of the novel is an impressive witness to the detailed and painstaking work that lies behind the book.

Richard is sent to live in Burgh Castle as the ward of the powerful Earl of Kent, Hubert de Burgh, when he is only eight years old, a few weeks older than de Burgh's daughter Meggotta. Their close relationship is crushed like a butterfly between the mighty forces that surround them. The capriciousness of King Henry III and the tension between the English barons and the avaricious Poitevan courtiers who infiltrate the Court create an atmosphere of mistrust and fear. The downfall of de Burgh and his ruthless persecution by Henry makes the rest of the baronage fear for their rights, and this struggle for power forms the background to the intimate story of the children. Richard and Meggotta are both heirs to great estates and their marriages would be expected to bring substantial gains to the families involved. For noble families, marriage was a business prospect and little else. Today we find it surprising that children were exchanged like inanimate objects and that a marriage could be conducted and consummated when the bride was only thirteen. Pargeter gives further thought to arranged marriages in several of the Cadfael novels, although none of her characters are of such high station as Richard and Meggotta.

Henry's arbitrary rule can morally destroy those who serve him and even de Burgh is eventually reduced to abandoning his loyalty to his wife and daughter. Those who stood out against the king's tyranny were unusual enough to be written into history by the actual chroniclers of the time, such as the blacksmith who refused to place iron fetters on the Earl of Kent and was noted by the Tewkesbury annalist. The names of the two young men who rescued de Burgh from captivity in Devizes Castle are recorded in the Close Rolls of Henry III.

The Marriage of Meggotta is the last of Pargeter's historical novels, and ranks with her finest achievements in that mode. The balance between the individual and the state is always shading the action and through the perspicacious eyes of Margaret, Meggotta's mother, the reader is brought to share in all the fears and alarms of life under an irrational monarch. Although the fate of Richard and Meggotta is always what engages the reader a genuine sense of a political world that affects even the humblest in the land gives the novel a solidity and redolence that sets it far apart from the category of romantic fiction.

Today, few historians continue to adopt the nineteenth century view of history as consisting only of verifiable facts. The facts may be there, but even they are open to differing interpretations. As R.R. Davies observed recently, there are many gaps between the facts, and the people who are most skilled at filling them in are often writers of fiction, not historians. They are the ones who can give the sense of what it was like to live in a certain period and to possess a certain cast of mind. In the writer's corner, the novelist J.G. Farrell held the same opinion, if somewhat more sceptically than the historians themselves:

> It is a common misconception that when the historians have finished with an historical incident there remains nothing but a patch of feathers and a pair of feet; in fact, the most important things, for the very reason that they are trivial, are unsuitable for digestion by historians, who are only able to nourish themselves on the signing of treaties, battle strategies, the formation of shadow Cabinets and so forth. These matters are quite alien to the life most people lead, which consists of catching colds, falling in love, or falling off bicycles. It is this real life which is the novelist's concern (though, needless to say, realism is not the only way to represent it).

The state of the historical novel is healthier than it has been for many years. Neil McEwan writing in his critical study *Perspective in British*

A TURBULENT HISTORY

Historical Fiction Today (1987) accords to historical novelists the role of humanists: 'they believe in an essential human nature to be discovered within the features of any particular culture.' They also find a position where continuity with the past is a crucial feature:

> They see a continuity with the past, in history, in literature, and in 'real people, who remain much the same', as Burgess says, and life which 'itself does not change very much', as Farrell says. This is a coherent position, and one which is under attack. To show the continuity, while acknowledging the extent to which life has changed, is itself a creative practice at the present time. (p.177)

It is also a position from which to launch a new kind of historical figure, and one which accords very much with this interpretation of human society. The figure of a medieval monk as detective is going to prove again and again just how contiguous the present and the past can be, even though in this case the difference in time is over eight hundred years.

6. The Cadfael World

I say more: the just man justices;
Keeps grace: that keeps all his goings graces;
Acts in God's eye what in God's eye he is —
Christ — for Christ plays in ten thousand places.
'As kingfishers catch fire' by Gerard Manley Hopkins

There is little doubt that Edith Pargeter and Ellis Peters would have proceeded very comfortably along on a pleasant and untroubled fictional journey had not the sturdy figure of Cadfael ap Meilyr ap Dafydd pushed his way into the affairs of the Abbey of St Peter and St Paul in Shrewsbury in the autumn of 1120. The combination of history and detection, the 'history and mystery' so beloved of American readers, was to prove an overwhelming popular success.

The development of the detective novel in the twentieth century has allowed for amateur sleuths from various walks of life to become successful at solving crimes; often more successfully than the professionals involved. The most famous of these is, of course, Sherlock Holmes, who haunted the dark streets of London at the turn of the century and who, for many people, still provides the classic tale of crime and detection. Another amateur who has grown in popularity in recent years, largely thanks to excellent BBC television versions of the novels, is Agatha Christie's Miss Marple, who does her sleuthing in conditions of extreme gentility in the south of England.

The first of the priestly detectives, G.K. Chesterton's Father Brown, emerged shortly after Sherlock Holmes. Chesterton published his first volume of short stories (*The Innocence of Father Brown*) featuring this unprepossessing Roman Catholic priest in 1911. Respected novelist and critic Julian Symons writing in *Bloody Murder* regards these stories highly: 'the best of these tales are among the finest short crime stories ever written' (p.78), and Oxford academic T.J. Binyon finds in his book *'Murder Will Out': The Detective in Fiction* that 'the best of the stories are undoubted masterpieces, brilliantly and poetically written, with the plot often turning on an ingenious, original paradox' (pp. 64-65). Unlike Cadfael, Father Brown's experience of life is limited to listening to the confessions of parishioners in his church, but this gives him a keen understanding of criminal psychology. Part of the reader's pleasure arises from the apparent contrast between the physical appearance of Father Brown (short, plump, shabbily dressed, struggling with his umbrella and wearing a large flat hat like a halo) and his penetrating insight into the nature of evil.

Contemporary writers have continued to find attractions in the role of the priest detective. The American priest Father Andrew M. Greeley has written many novels featuring his series character the Reverend Monsignor 'Blackie' Ryan, Rector of Holy Name Cathedral in Chicago and he has acquired a high reputation for the moral and religious content of his work.

Crime-solving should not be considered as the exclusive preserve of the priestly fraternity, however, as nuns have proved to be just as adept at unravelling mysteries. Sister Carol Anne O'Marie, who has been a nun for forty years, bases her Sister Mary Helen mysteries on the principal of a religious college whom she knew well, even to her practice of reading mystery novels tucked into a prayer-book cover. Katherine Hall Page has a series of novels featuring the minister's wife as sleuth, and English novelists Catherine Aird and Antonia Fraser have both set mysteries in convents: Aird published *The Religious Body* in 1966, and Fraser published *Quiet as a Nun* in 1977. Across the Channel, in 1950s France, novelist Henri Catalan was exploring the unexpected interests of the observant Soeur Angèle of the Sisters of Charity, who, armed with a useful degree in Legal Medicine from the University of Paris, an umbrella and a large handbag manages to solve three intricate murders.

The arrival of the first Cadfael manuscript at Macmillan's office in 1976 did not create a stir. According to her editor of many years, George Hardinge, neither her agent nor her publishers realised what they held. Peters herself had just finished writing a modern crime novel *Never Pick Up Hitch-Hikers!* (1976) and a major series of historical novels. *A Morbid Taste for Bones* was written as a one-off, to fill a gap in a tightly-packed schedule and was immediately followed by *Rainbow's End*, which turned out to be the final Felse novel. The first

Brother Cadfael novel was published only in hardback, with a modest run of 5,000 copies, largely for library sales. But the plot of a succeeding novel had fallen into Peters's lap as she looked through the history of Shrewsbury and thought about the seige of the town in August 1138, a year after the relics of St Winifred had been brought to the abbey. From that point on, Cadfael began to assume a life of his own, and, said Peters, 'there was no turning back.' If the emergence of Brother Cadfael and his world appears to be fortuitous, not to say 'star-crossed', it is not an unreasonable conclusion to reach. For a sixty-four year old writer suddenly to find new inspiration and to follow it as instinctively as Peters did is both unusual and particularly satisfying.

The publishing history of Ellis Peters during the late 1970s is very revealing. She had parted company with Heinemann because they had allowed the first volume of *The Heaven Tree* trilogy to go out of print before the third was even published; infuriating to a novelist who always sees this as being her finest piece of work. The first Cadfael novels continued to be issued in hardback by Macmillan but sales were modest and appreciation was limited. Her agent Deborah Owen was frustrated but Peters was not. Owen told Stephen Pile in an interview published in the *Sunday Telegraph* Magazine that 'lack of success did not eat her up. It did not bother her because she had inner peace. It bothered me. But she knew she was a good writer and did not have to prove herself to anyone.'

Owen feels sure that despite Peters's reservations about the book, the concept of the medieval mystery was widened and strengthened by Umberto Eco's intellectual tour de force *The Name of the Rose*, which was published in 1980 in Italian and 1983 in English translation. Some aficionados of crime fiction found Eco's use of Conan Doyle a reassuring confirmation of the place of genre fiction in the development of the novel, but Eco was clearly exploiting the tools of detective fiction for his own dazzling purposes. Although many were impressed, many also found Eco's parading of knowledge to be arrogant and his mystification of the reader to be intensely irritating. Ellis Peters has always been reluctant to read books which overlap with her own period, and even though Eco's novel is set two hundred years later than the Cadfael Chronicles she resisted reading it for some time. When she eventually did so, she felt that the rights of the reader had been somewhat betrayed:

I thought it marred by the inclusion of lengthy passages in Latin, without any concession to those who have not that language, and by the fact that he makes no mention of his title until the last line of the book, and then in Latin, so that the rose of yesteryear and its lingering influence as a name is lost on many readers. I find it unkind and unfair to market a book, from the full understanding and enjoyment of which a substantial part of the readership is excluded.

Little wonder that Peters's hackles rose when her paperback publisher Futura unfortunately used the phrase 'in the tradition of *The Name of the Rose*' in some publicity material — 'seven of my books had been published before Eco's first', she remarked crisply in an interview in *The Guardian*. Andrew Greeley, writing in *The Armchair Detective* in March 1985 found her 'a far better storyteller than Umberto Eco,' and this is undoubedly true, but it must also be recognised that Eco did not have this as his major aim in constructing the novel.

Deborah Owen feels that ultimately the huge international success of *The Name of the Rose* was beneficial to the Cadfael series. Although Eco was writing about a period two hundred years later than Cadfael, attention was still being focused on a medieval monastery and its monks. Up to then, says Owen dryly, 'the medieval period had not been appreciated by certain marketing men.' But now readers of Eco brought an unexpected appetite for the medieval period in all its aspects, and Peters's meticulously researched novels were suddenly in demand. At last, after several years of trying, Owen secured a substantial paperback contract for the Cadfael novels with Futura. Many sad editors deeply regret having declined this opportunity.

The enormous success of the Chronicles of Brother Cadfael can be ascribed to a number of different features and it is worth spending some time establishing how skilfully Peters has assembled and used her material. The historical setting, the border tensions, the sense of community surrounding the abbey, the abbey and its brethren, the creation of a credible group of developing characters, including Cadfael himself, the peaceful and fragrant garden within the abbey walls, the passage of the seasons and finally the subtle presence of a Christian faith that is lived every minute of the day are blended together to produce novels of considerable sophistication.

Undoubtedly the firm texture of the Cadfael Chronicles depends very much on the strong sense of community that Peters creates, both within and outside the abbey walls. The novels are chronological, beginning in 1137 and continuing in careful sequence. Peters has found the structure of the novels very dependent on this placing in time as well as locale and told Mike Ashley in an interview published in *Million* that:

> The steady progression of the books has surprised me... It has caused me to lay emphasis on season, weather and the relig-ious sequence of the year. But as soon as I realised this, I recognised how appropriate it is, since we are concerned with the regular lives of a community, people who make their exits and entrances in my books, but live just as surely in the intervals, and are dependent on times and seasons. (p.10)

Crucially important also is the convincing way in which actual historical events are woven into the fictions that she creates. The plots themselves derive largely from the apparently dry-as-dust pages of historical chronicles. The entire Cartulary (register) of Shrewsbury Abbey was edited and published by the National Library of Wales in 1975 and Peters uses this as a source of extensive detail about the seasonal work of a great religious house, both spiritual and practical. Beyond the abbey gates the events connected with the unsettled monarchy during the middle years of the twelfth century, known in historical terms as 'The Anarchy', provide a strong background of national and even international tensions against which the affairs of humbler men can be placed. In the story 'A Light on the Road to Woodstock' for instance, a trial in a local court is delayed for three days because the king's only legitimate son has been shipwrecked and drowned off the coast of Normandy. This gives Cadfael an opportunity to free an imprisoned prior and to see that the true path of justice is followed. The clash of the followers of King Stephen and the supporters of his rival the Empress Maud is a recurrent backdrop to the quiet rhythm of abbey life, when hard-rid-ing messengers from north or south can burst into the abbey yard bringing news of cruel defeats and ephemeral triumphs in the struggle for the throne.

Peters always gets her history right — 'you must respect doc-umented fact — only when the authorities fight over details do I use my own judgement and make a mix with fiction.' As a result her novels find their way on to the reading lists of history courses in

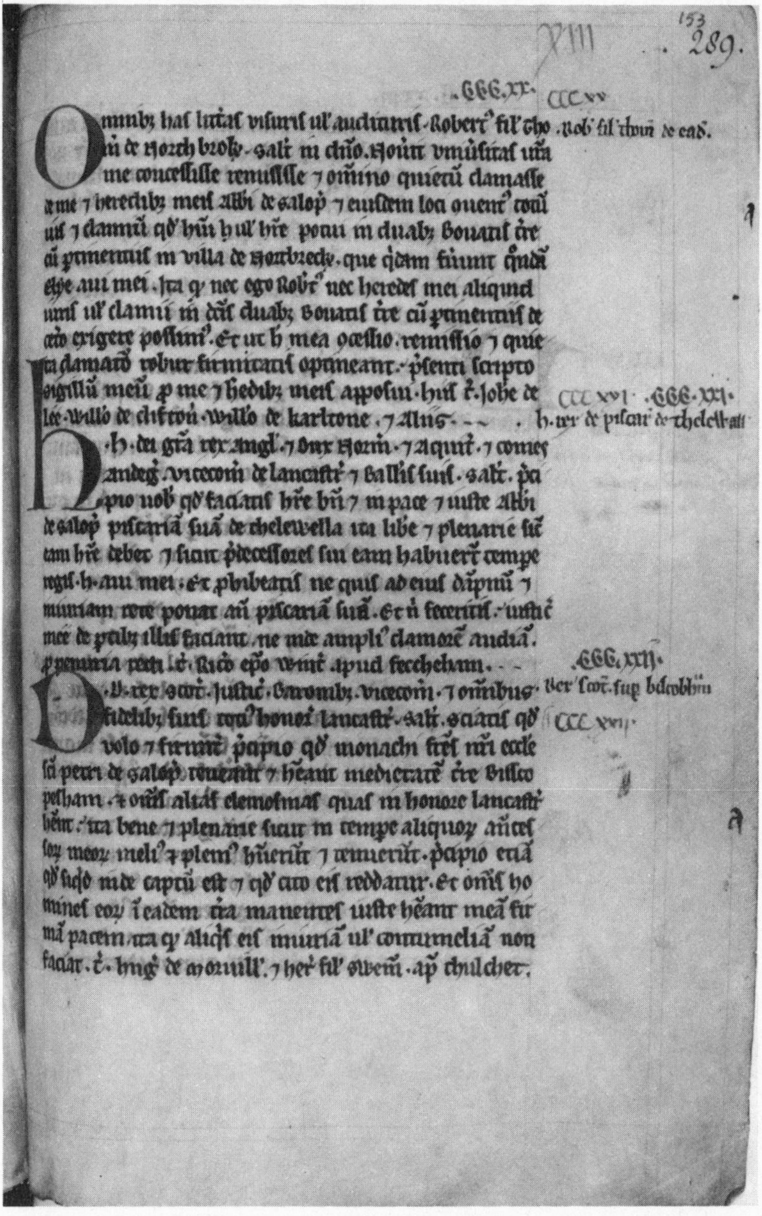

A page from the Cartulary of Shrewsbury Abbey

British universities. History professors accept Peters's creation of a medieval world that functions on its own terms. By removing her location from the centre of power to the Borders the author can be sparing with actual political detail, providing just enough to give a realistic sense of a world of affairs whose influence can still affect even the smallest corners of the unhappy kingdom. The details that she incorporates are carefully checked but historical accuracy would amount to very little if the characters in her novels were not interesting and attractive. The approval of the academics is, however, encouraging for a professional who has always taken pride in her historical reliability.

Nothing in the first Cadfael novel, *A Morbid Taste for Bones,* creates conflict with the books that follow; indeed, the establishment of the abbey and its surroundings, the personalities of the individual brothers and the life of the town of Shrewsbury are clearly depicted from the outset and no substantial alterations take place during twenty novels written between 1977 and 1994. The reader's understanding of the cloistered world within the abbey gates contrasted to the commercial bustle of the streets beyond and the constant awareness of being a Border stronghold is expanded with each novel, so that our familiarity with the period increases and we feel more and more at ease in time and place.

Shrewsbury's closeness to the border between England and Wales is a crucial factor in most of the Cadfael Chronicles. Welsh law and English law differed a great deal, since even William the Conqueror had failed to impose Norman legal forms on the unruly principalities beyond the Marches. In John Davies's *History of Wales* the difference between the two legal systems is elegantly defined:

> The Law is among the most splendid creations of the culture of the Welsh. For centuries it was a powerful symbol of their unity and identity, as powerful indeed as their language, for — like the literary language — the Law was the same in its essence in all parts of Wales. The Law of Hywel was not a body of law created *de novo* ; it was the systematization of the legal customs which had developed in Wales over the centuries. The Law of Wales, therefore, was folk law rather than state law and its emphasis was upon ensuring reconciliation between kinship groups rather than upon keeping order through punishment. It was not concerned with the enforcement of criminal law through the apparatus of the state...it

contained elements of mercy, common sense and respect for women and children which would be lacking in the Law of England until very recently. (p.88)

Little wonder that the flexibility and subtlety of King Hywel's Laws appealed to Brother Cadfael rather more than the strictly defined Norman codes which bound the sheriff Hugh Beringar, and it is no surprise that Cadfael is often the instrument of achieving mysterious disappearances across the border.

The Chronicles are not unique in leaning on the presence of a border to find definition. The 'Iron Curtain' between eastern and western Europe, for instance, particularly the harsh physical intrusion of the Berlin Wall which divided the city, provided a backdrop for many thrillers. To escape across the border meant freedom, just as fugitives fleeing from justice in the United States frequently head for the Mexican border. Almost always the guilty in Cadfael's world speed westwards along quiet forest paths to reach Wales, only about ten miles away. Sometimes they are successful, as in *Dead Man's Ransom*, but not always. The sheriff also knows these forest paths and some fugitives are brought back to face their crimes. On occasion, the prospect of escape is offered but not taken until a name can be cleared and innocence established. The feudal system of villeinage or even slavery could propel independent-minded young men and women towards the more humane laws of Wales. For any number of reasons, the presence of a territorial border plays an important role in the development of the narratives, providing a psychological as well as a physical boundary of mountain and dyke.

The plot of the first Cadfael novel requires the central character to be Welsh, since he accompanies the deputation of clerics who go to Wales to secure the bones of St Winifred for Shrewsbury Abbey and acts as interpreter between the Welsh villagers and the monks. This is a role that Brother Cadfael can ably fulfil since he was born in Trefriw, Gwynedd, and has relatives scattered across most of North Wales. But there is perhaps another, more personal reason for making Cadfael Welsh. Peters has always valued her Welsh grandmother and finds the Celtic race endlessly romantic; 'the Welsh are more exotic', she has said. She rightly sees the Welsh as being very different from the English today, and they were certainly very different from the Norman French in the twelfth century.

Cadfael needed other qualities as well as his fluency in the Welsh language: 'my monk had to be a man of wide worldy experience and an inexhaustible fund of resigned tolerance for the human condition.' Even in the first novel there are strong suggestions that Cadfael has had an unusual past, and his experience of men and their motives fits him very well for his role as what his creator has called 'the high medieval equivalent of a detective, an observer and agent of justice in the centre of the action.' As the novels unfold so does his past, revealing that Cadfael had not been an ascetic by any means. In *Monk's-Hood* he meets a former love, Richildis, whom he had left after plighting his affection, and in *The Virgin in the Ice* he is astonished to find that he is facing a son that he never knew he had, product of a happy liaison with Mariam, the dark-haired young widow who sold fruit and vegetables in the Street of the Sailmakers in Antioch. For Cadfael had been a Crusader, having left unprofitable service with a wool merchant in Shrewsbury and answered the call of Pope Urban II to Christians everywhere to defeat the aggressive Seljuk Turks and to ensure the safety of the Holy Sepulchre at Jerusalem. Young Cadfael heard it as a call to adventure, and he was among the army of the First Crusade led by Godfrey de Bouillon who stormed and took Antioch in 1098. The following year he took part in the six-week seige and battle for Jerusalem. The city was taken on 15 July 1099, and all the inhabitants were slaughtered. This is the battle that haunts Cadfael as he dozes behind his pillar in the Chapter House of Shrewsbury Abbey, many years later:

> The heat of the sun rebounded from honed facets of pale, baked rock, scorching his face, as the floating arid dust burned his throat. From where he crouched with his fellows in cover he could see the long crest of the wall, and the steel-capped heads of the guards on the turrets glittering in the fierce light. A landscape carved out of reddish stone and fire, all deep gullies and sheer cliffs with never a cool green leaf to temper it, and before him the object of all his journeyings, the holy city of Jerusalem, crowned with towers and domes within its white walls. The dust of battle hung in the air, dimming the clarity of battlement and gate, and the hoarse shouting and clashing of armour filled his ears. He was waiting for the trumpet to sound the final assault, and keeping well in cover while he waited, for he had learned to respect the range of the short, curly Saracen bow. He saw the banners surge forward out of hiding, streaming on the burning wind. He saw the

flash of the raised trumpet, and braced himself for the blare. (p.15)

After Jerusalem had been secured Cadfael ended his military career on land and became a ship's captain for ten years, sailing the Eastern Mediterranean and waging continual war against the Infidel. Eventually he returned to Normandy where King Henry I had been consolidating his hold, and joined the forces of Roger Mauduit as man-at-arms before accompanying him back to England. As he rides his own mount from the channel to Roger Mauduit's manor in Northampton — 'a broad-set, sturdy, muscular man in his healthy prime, brown-haired and brown-skinned from eastern suns and outdoor living, well-provided in leather coat and good cloth, and well-armed with sword and dagger. A comely enough face, strongly featured, with the bold bones of his race' — he is aware that his life is balanced at a point of change. Peters describes his position as 'the acceptance of a revelation from within that the life he has lived to date, active, mobile and often violent, has reached its natural end, and he is confronted by a new need and a different challenge.' The old soldier lays his sword on the steps of the altar of the parish church of St Mary Magdalene at Woodstock and embarks on a new life as a Benedictine brother, 'like a battered ship settling at last for a quiet harbour.' The incident is not described until the short story called 'A Light on the Road to Woodstock', written in 1985 and published in the collection *A Rare Benedictine* in 1988.

Reflecting on his decision to take monastic vows many years after this event, Cadfael is satisfied with the change in his life and we are told in *A Morbid Taste for Bones* that:

> Brother Cadfael himself found nothing strange in his wide-ranging career, and had forgotten nothing and regretted nothing. He saw no contradiction in the delight he had taken in battle and adventure, and the keen pleasure he now found in quietude. Spiced, to be truthful, with more than a little mischief when he could get it, as he liked his victuals well-flavoured, but quietude all the same, a ship becalmed and enjoying it. (p.10)

The secure, well-regulated life of the Benedictine Brothers at the Abbey of St Peter and St Paul in Shrewsbury underlies all the novels. The Benedictine Order had been introduced to England after the

Norman Conquest in 1066. Roger of Montgomery, who was created Earl of Shrewsbury in 1074, brought French monks to re-establish monasticism in Shropshire. The ancient religious house of Much Wenlock had been founded in 690 for monks and nuns by the Mercian king Merewald, and his daughter Milburga was the first abbess. She later became a saint and the veneration of her relics led Prior Robert of Shrewsbury to search for an equally powerful patron for his own abbey, which was nearby. Much Wenlock had declined and become a secular community long before the Norman invasion, and it was re-established as a Cluniac House in about 1079. Near at hand, a Savigniac House was founded at Buildwas, on the banks of the Severn. A stone-built abbey was begun in 1135 and it was eventually completed in 1200. The ruins of this building, which was partly demolished during the dissolution, are still very impressive and as with most abbeys built at that time, it is surrounded by rich and beautiful scenery. Earl Roger also dedicated himself to the building of the Abbey of St Peter and St Paul in Shrewsbury, and he died three days after being received into the brotherhood as a monk, in 1094. His tomb was placed between the two altars of a sparkling new building, at a time when church and state were seen to be growing in power and prosperity.

Shrewsbury remained an independent Benedictine Abbey with a less ascetic regime than some of the newer foundations. The rule of St Benedict of Nursia (died c.550) formed the basis for a huge expansion in monasticism throughout the Middle Ages. His order did not make unreasonable demands on his followers, as R.H.C. Davis explains in *A History of Medieval Europe:*

> On entering a religious community a Benedictine monk re-nounced the world. He vowed to surrender all his private property, to obey the abbot in all things, and not to leave the monastery until he died. The aim of his life was to practise Christian humility by humbling himself before his superiors, by working in the fields, and by giving the glory to God. The most important of his duties was the *opus Dei* or 'work of God' — the proper performance of the church services for which St Benedict had offered such precise liturgical instructions. (p.251)

The monastic world is restricted, but from this apparently narrow focus a microcosm of society in twelfth century Shrewsbury emerges. The regular pattern of services comprised seven offices beginning with Matins at midnight, almost immediately followed by Lauds and a return to the dortoir or dormitory. The first office of the day was Prime, at dawn, then Terce (about nine o'clock), Sext (about noon), Nones in the middle of the afternoon at three o'clock, Vespers in the late afternoon, and Compline before the community retired for the night. Other Masses would have been held during the day for the townspeople and lay workers to attend. This daily pattern was fundamental to St Benedict's Rule, which emphasised regular prayer, worship and study. But it still left time to engage in all the other activities of the community, such as making books, teaching young pupils and preparing music for services, as well as working in the fields and abbey gardens. Time was needed to administer the abbey's substantial agricultural estates and the property it owned in the town. Shrewsbury Abbey held the mono-poly on corn-milling and, through tithes and other taxes, contrived to ensure a handsome income.

Abbey estates were usually well-managed in the twelfth and thirteenth centuries and the Abbots themselves were men of consid-erable ability, a spiritual elite with managerial and political acumen. By the end of the fourteenth century, however, standards had de-clined seriously. Shrewsbury Abbey was dissolved in 1540 and the property was confiscated by the Crown. Even so, it was nineteenth century road-builders, not Thomas Cromwell, who did most dam-age to the remaining abbey buildings, and left the nave stranded in an island of busy roads instead of at the centre of an integrated community of religious and lay workers, surrounded by gardens and cultivated fields as it was in Cadfael's time.

This strong sense of community contributes powerfully to the success of the Cadfael Chronicles. The character of Cadfael is obviously crucial, but so also is the depiction of his friends and colleagues. The brothers of Shrewsbury Abbey allow Peters a wide canvas of human foibles to draw on. The notion of a rigidly control-led body of men who have lost their individuality on taking the cloth could not be farther from her intentions. Each member of the order is characterised and described, and they develop in succeeding novels. Abbot Heribert rules the abbey during the first three novels, to be replaced by Abbot Radulfus because he wavered politically at the wrong time. Heribert 'was old, of mild nature and pliant, a gentle grey ascetic very wishful of peace and harmony around him. His figure was unimpressive, though his face was beguiling in its anxious sweetness. Novices and pupils were easy in his presence, when they could reach it...' Radulfus proves to be 'both an austere but just disciplinarian and a shrewd and strong-minded business-man.' He is tall, with a lean hatchet face and a penetrating gaze. Although he values Cadfael's unique qualities, and willingly allows his brother to miss one of the offices when given good reason, Cadfael often feels that his excuses are transparent before the Abbot's sharp eyes, and that his errands outside the abbey walls are tolerated only because the Abbot also feels that justice sometimes needs a helping hand.

Very different is the cleric next in seniority, Prior Robert Pennant. Peters emphasises his commanding presence, tall, silver-haired, aristocratic and ambitious. Having confidently expected to be made abbot in place of Heribert, he is disappointed to be denied this powerful position. We are never in any doubt that his judgement is always more superficial than that of Radulfus. The sub-Prior, Brother Richard, shares neither Robert's qualities nor his ambitions: 'large, ungainly, amiable and benevolent, of a good mind, but mentally lazy.' He comes from farming stock and shows his best qualities when advising on the cultivation of the abbey's farms.

Other figures have their parts clearly defined. Brother Jerome, Prior Robert's clerk, is scrupulous in his observance of his duties and seems to derive an immodest pride in reporting the failings of others to his superior: 'A meagre man in the flesh was Brother Jerome, but he made up for it in zeal, though there were those who found that zeal too narrowly channelled, and somewhat dehydrated of the milk of human tolerance.' Naturally he and Cadfael fare best when their paths do not cross, but even so it is a shock when Jerome's extreme piety turns to violence in *The Holy Thief*.

Brother Paul, master of the novices, is a favourite of Cadfael. As teacher and mentor to the boys at the abbey school he is kind and functions as a guide, not a goad; creating a happy and disciplined atmosphere. His good qualities are not to be construed as weakness, however, and he is well able to defend his charges when the need arises.

Other essential offices in the life of the abbey are held by Brother Anselm, the precentor, and Brother Edmund, the infirmarer. Anselm is a musician — 'a vague, slender, short-sighted person who peered beneath an untidy brown tonsure and bristling brows to match, and smiled amiably and encouragingly.' Not only does he lead the chants for regular services, he takes a great deal of interest in music of all kinds. He is not averse to giving a new lease of life to a secular love song by writing a new setting for a religious purpose. The hunted jongleur in *The Sanctuary Sparrow* is treated kindly by Brother Anselm, who patiently helps him to restore the smashed rebec that he lost while being pursued by a vengeful mob.

Brother Edmund, who is in charge of the infirmary, works closely with Brother Cadfael. Here sick brothers are brought back to health and the elderly are allowed to spend their final years in peace and comfort. Edmund is competent and devoted to his office. He is sensitive to the often unspoken needs of those he tends; like Cadfael he is a careful observer of human nature.

The duties of the hospitaller, Brother Dennis, vary as to the season. The abbey, as with most monastic houses, offers hospitality to travellers as part of its Christian duty. Rich and poor alike would be given food and shelter without charge, although it was customary for the wealthy to leave a gift. He is responsible for all the provisions that extra guests need at Christmas time, at St Peter's Fair and at the Feast celebrating the translation of St Winifred to the abbey. Brother Dennis is distinguished by his ability to recall the faces of the visitors that have passed through the abbey halls as we learn in *The Pilgrim of Hate*:

> Brother Dennis had a retentive memory and an appetite for news and rumours that usually kept him the best-informed person in the enclave. The fuller his halls, the more pleasure he took in knowing everything that went on there, and the name and vocation of every guest. He also kept meticulous books to record the visitations. (p.184)

Such a source of well-documented information as to the comings and goings of strangers is often invaluable to Cadfael and to the sheriff in untangling the strands of a crime.

Cadfael has little to do with Brother Matthew, the cellarer, who looks after wine and provisions, since he takes care of his own supply of wine, nor with Brother Benedict the sacristan who was responsible for the upkeep of the church and the grounds. But Brother Petrus, the cook, is someone that he deals with regularly, as supplier of herbs and spices, fruits and vegetables for the abbey kitchen. Petrus is 'a red-haired and belligerent northerner' and 'a cook of pride and honour'. He loathes Prior Robert, yet his pride will only allow him to express his feelings by making a dish so exceptionally rich and well-flavoured that the Prior may not be able to stomach it. Brother Oswald, the silversmith, takes the role of almoner and has important links with the town as a result. Two of Cadfael's apprentices, the shock-haired Brother Mark and the cheerful but clumsy Brother Oswin, go on to take charge of the sick at the hospice of St Giles. Brother Mark later finds his vocation as a priest. Brother Rhun, subject of a blessing by St Winifred, is also sure of his priestly role and brings a shining image of human goodness wherever he goes.

Historical records indicate that the actual establishment of monks at most abbeys was relatively small, but a large group of lay brethren would have served an abbey and its estates. During most of the Middle Ages the number of clerics at Shrewsbury varied from twelve to eighteen brethren. Of those only a few would be priests; Cadfael himself is not and is not empowered to hear confession or to deliver the Sacraments.

The main contact with the life of Shrewsbury is through Hugh Beringar of Maesbury, at first deputy sheriff and then sheriff. The office of sheriff was a crucial one to the government of the country. Appointed by the king they were responsible only to him, and provided the most important tier of district government. Beringar is half Cadfael's age but his shrewd mind is generally in close accord with his friend in the cloister. Unlike the Abbot and the Prior, whose names are recorded in the records of the abbey (though not their personal characteristics — for this we must reach into the realms of Peters's imagination), Beringar is entirely a fictional creation: 'I was free to fill the vacancy,' said Peters in an interview. He appears in the second chronicle, *One Corpse Too Many*, offering his services to King Stephen: a 'bold and possibly over-fluent young man'; in appearance 'a lightweight, not above the middle height and slenderly built, but of balanced and assured movement; he might well make up in speed and agility what he lacked in bulk and reach. Perhaps two or three years past twenty, black-avised, with thin, alert features and thick, quirky dark brows. An unchancy fellow, because there was no guessing from his face what went on behind the deep-set eyes.'

At first Cadfael regards Beringar with suspicion and they test each other throughout their initial encounter, but Hugh and his new bride Aline soon become familiar inhabitants of Cadfael's world. To Hugh he entrusts his closest secrets, such as the identity of his son, and the complex story of the bones of St Winifred. Cadfael is further bound to Hugh and Aline by becoming godfather to their son Giles, born at Christmas in 1139.

Within the town other characters play a regular part, such as Madog, the boatman, whose knowledge of the river Severn as it loops around the peninsula on which the town is built proves invaluable on several occasions. Other townspeople are developed to suit the plot, and Peters is meticulous in her research into clothing, housing, food and craft work. She dislikes the word research, however, maintaining in her interview with Mike Ashley that 'it suggests hard work, and I could happily spend every moment buried among books in the archives. It isn't work at all, it's pure pleasure. But I do respect every known and agreed fact, and I do consider it vital to seek out every last authority. It's half the pleasure to win without cheating.'

It is essential that the reader be totally confident in this created world, resting as it does on actual historical events. As the novelist Jane Aiken Hodge has pointed out in her essay 'Writing Historical Novels' published in *Techniques of Novel Writing*:

> The constant interplay between the real and the imaginary time-scheme adds enormously to the stress, and consequently to the satisfaction of the writing. The whole business is delightfully full of setbacks and surprises, and it is a rare book that ends as one has planned. But when it comes to the crunch, fiction must always give way to fact. If you betray your reader once, he will never trust you again.(p.224)

Despite the necessary limitations of novels centred on the set routine of abbey life, with the central figure of a Benedictine monk, the novels all contain an important romantic element. Typically, young lovers are thwarted and have to overcome adversity, proving themselves worthy of each other in a trial of strength and resolution. It is interesting to note how often strong women direct the path of true love and seem set to carry on directing the relationship once it is firmly established. Beautiful they often are, but ethereal they are not; these women know how to make their way bravely in the world. Cadfael is invariably sympathetic to young couples and the abbot seems to share profound views about arranged marriages that are designed only to consolidate land and power.

Cadfael often finds it useful to turn to a sympathetic and experienced woman in working out satisfactory resolutions to entangled relationships, and he finds such a friend in Avice of Thornbury, the former mistress of a Norman baron, who in middle age joins an order of Benedictine nuns — 'she had put off all her finery as an old soldier retiring might put off arms, as no longer of use or interest to him, and turn his considerable energies to farming.' And indeed, when Cadfael first sees her she is efficiently planting out young cabbages in the convent garden, 'pressing the soil firm around her transplants with a broad foot, and brushing the loam from her hands with placid satisfaction.' Avice, whose renunciation of the world is not dissimilar to Cadfael's own, is able to help him on a number of occasions where strict adherence to the Benedictine Rule is slightly at odds with the desired resolution of human problems.

Peters has admitted that she does indeed have 'a soft spot for the young' which she passes on to Brother Cadfael. She has suggested in an article written for *Fifty Plus Magazine* that this comes through growing old and developing tolerance and generosity with maturing years, but the evidence of her earlier fiction shows that she has always liked to write about young people. Dominic Felse and his friends were given important roles in several novels and even her early, pre-war romances give special prominence to the emotional intensity felt by people on the brink of maturity.

Brother Cadfael is able to help overcome so many barriers in the way of young lovers because he himself is remarkably mobile and independent, while still doing his best to obey the rules of his order. Content though he generally is within his empire Cadfael occasionally feels the desire to revert to the state of the 'vagus', the wanderer, and he is grateful that his special skills allow him to move beyond the abbey walls to tend the sick in the town and in the manors and farms which make up the abbey estates. His abilities as a herbalist and healer take him into the tapestry-hung chambers of the rich and to the wretched dwellings of the poor. He provides sleeping draughts for highly-strung merchant's wives and soothing ointments for the lepers outside the walls. Less legitimate business, according to the strictures of the Rule, develops when Cadfael's nose scents a crime, particularly when suspicion is cast on someone whom he feels to be innocent. When the offices of the day conflict with detection Cadfael suffers some guilt, but not usually a great deal. We catch a sudden glimpse of this near the end of *The Hermit of Eyton Forest* when Cadfael is riding back to Shrewsbury with Hugh Beringar after setting to rights another complex mystery. He is suddenly

overcome with remorse as to the relish with which he has undertaken the challenge:

> They rode home together in the deepening dusk, as they had
> so often ridden together since first they encountered in wary
> contention, wit against wit, and came to a gratifying stand at
> the end of the match, fast friends. The night was still and mild,
> the morning would be misty again, the lush valley fields a
> translucent blue sea. The forest smelled of autumn, ripe, moist
> earth, bursting fungus, the sweet, rich rot of leaves.
>
> 'I have transgressed against my vocation,' said Cadfael, at
> once solaced and saddened by the season and the hour. 'I
> know it. I undertook the monastic life, but now I am not sure
> I could support it without you, without these stolen excur-
> sions outside the walls. For so they are. True, I am often sent
> upon legitimate labours here without, but also I steal, I take
> more than is my due by right. Worse, Hugh, I do not repent
> me! Do you suppose there is room within the bounds of grace
> for one who has set his hand to the plough, and every little
> while abandons his furrow to turn back among the sheep and
> lambs?'
>
> 'I think the sheep and lambs might think so,' said Hugh,
> gravely smiling. 'He would have their prayers. Even the black
> sheep and the grey, like some you've argued for against God
> and me in your time.'
>
> 'There are very few all black,' said Cadfael. 'Dappled,
> perhaps, like this great rangy beast you choose to ride. Most
> of us have a few mottles about us. As well, maybe, it makes
> for a more tolerant judgement of the rest of God's creatures.
> But I have sinned, and most of all in relishing my sin. I shall
> do penance by biding dutifully within the walls through the
> winter, unless I'm sent forth, and then I'll make haste with my
> task and hurry back.'
>
> 'Until the next waif stumbles across your path.'(pp. 210-11)

Hugh is understandably sceptical, because he knows that Cadfael's
insatiable curiosity about human nature is likely to overcome even
his best intentions, as indeed it does. In not many months time he
will be accompanying a contrite pilgrim on a long and arduous
journey (*The Confession of Brother Haluin*) and will be unravelling
another mystery.

Cadfael's knowledge of healing has been gathered up during his
many years as soldier and sailor in the Middle East. Not only is he

able to use his herbal medicines effectively, he knows how to dress serious wounds (*An Excellent Mystery*) and how to relieve cramped muscles through massage (*The Pilgrim of Hate*). He patiently reconstructs Brother Haluin's shattered legs in *The Confession of Brother Haluin* and he strives fruitlessly to save Gervase Bonel from the effects of poison in *Monk's-Hood*. In all his dealings with the sick and injured he brings comfort and understanding. Above all, he brings his own calm and uncomplicated faith that God's will and man's desires will ultimately flow together in the river of life.

Familiarity with Cadfael's fragrant garden grows during the course of the Chronicles, helped by useful sketch maps of the abbey and its environs in the novels where this is considered to be important. 'In these books the topography is as true as I can make it, with some speculation on the changes the centuries have made,' Peters has said. The seasons unfold not only in Cadfael's herb garden but also in the regular produce of the vegetable garden, which is nearer the guest-hall, and in the surrounding lands. Bringing in the valuable woolclip, gathering fruit in the orchards, harvesting the hay and even collecting firewood on the allotted days are all recorded and woven into the fabric of the novels. Weather is an important part of daily life and Peters treats it seriously, helping us to think about the practical problems of travelling in frost and snow, and in ensuring a continuous cycle of crops for the kitchen.

Neither should it be overlooked that the climatic period in which Cadfael sowed and reaped his crops was indeed favoured. The years between 1150 and 1300 were unusually warm and allowed the cultivation of vineyards as far north as York, as well as tender plants such as figs and ginger. The winter of 1142 was exceptionally cold, and enabled the Empress Maud to escape from the siege of Oxford over ice and snow, but generally speaking the twelfth century continued mild. This was followed by the 'little ice age' and vineyards had virtually disappeared by 1320. When Peters refers to the twelfth century as being a time of optimism, this surely relates, at least in part, to a general improvement in the gloom of English weather.

The herb garden is usefully located well away from the bustle of the gatehouse and court. In the middle stands Cadfael's garden shed, an essential apparatus in the working out of various complicated plots. Here runaways hide, illicit love affairs are promoted and confidential conversations of all kinds are exchanged. The shed fills up with dried herbs in autumn and bottles of wines and cordial are ranged on the shelves. When the charcoal brazier is lit on chilly days it is a cosy refuge for a brother who does not always seek out spiritual glory from prayer and contemplation, but is more likely to find God very naturally in the best qualities of humankind and in the peace and tranquillity of his garden.

As well as his medicines, which take the form of syrups, ointments and lozenges, all manufactured by Cadfael and his apprentice over the brazier in the garden hut, he makes more delicate preparations. His perfumed oils burn before the altar in the abbey church and also in the side chapels. These oils would have burned in small cresset lamps and would probably have been given fragrance with essence of lavender, rose petals and other flowers. Special care would have been given to the lamp on St Winifred's altar. His duties are described in *The Raven in the Foregate*:

> Cadfael had returned to the church after Prime to replenish the perfumed oil in the lamp on St Winifred's altar. The inquisitive skills which might have been frowned upon if they had been employed to make scents for women's vanity became permissible and even praiseworthy when used as an act of worship, and he took pleasure in trying out all manner of fragrant herbs and flowers in many different combinations, plying the sweets of rose and lily, violet and clover against the searching aromatic riches of rue and sage and wormwood. It pleased him to think that the lady must take delight in being so served, for virgin saint though she might be, she was a woman, and in her youth had been a beautiful and desirable one. (p.138)

Another task that Cadfael cheerfully undertakes in the bountiful days of summer is the making of wine. Some of this was medicinal, certainly — 'distilled with herbs, good for the blood and heart' — and designed to accompany an unpalatable draught, but a good store was laid by for companionable conversation in the privacy of his own domain, the garden hut. Hugh Beringar is particularly appreciative of a restorative glass after a long day in the saddle, and the meditative processes of monk and sheriff invariably benefit. It is fortunate for Cadfael that the more exemplary followers of the Rule, such as Brother Jerome, do not often venture into his territory, and Cadfael continues to use his wine store with judicious discretion.

Cadfael's duties also extended to the supervision of the kitchen gardens and the supply of herbs for the cook. Authorities on the medieval diet generally agree that meat and fish stored for long periods over the winter months needed robust flavouring to make it palatable. Peters does not supply much detail about the everyday meals consumed by the brothers, but certain special feasts are described at length, such as the Christmas celebration in *Monk's-Hood:*

> With the approach of Christmas it was quite usual for many of the merchants of Shrewsbury, and the lords of many small manors close by, to give a guilty thought to the welfare of their souls, and their standing as devout and ostentatious Christians, and to seek small ways of acquiring merit, preferably as economically as possible. The conventual fare of pulse, beans, fish and occasional and meagre meat, benefited by sudden gifts of flesh and fowl to provide treats for the monks of St Peter's. Honey-baked cakes appeared, and dried fruits, and chickens, and even, sometimes, a haunch of venison, all devoted to the pittances that turned a devotional sacrament into a rare indulgence, a holy day into a holiday. (p.388)

The fatal dish of plump partridge basted with rich wine sauce flavoured with rosemary and rue would certainly have derived its savoury aroma from Cadfael's herbs.

Peters has clearly spent many happy hours envisaging the interior of Cadfael's hut and she describes it with total conviction. The dried herbs, after hanging in bunches, are transferred to linen bags for storage. Poultices are pounded in a stone pestle and mortar. The utensils placed on the brazier are generally pottery and are prone to crack if a careless apprentice cools them too quickly. There are few glass containers and they tend to store poisons. When Cadfael loads up his scrip, or satchel, to visit the hospice and leper colony at St Giles, which he does regularly every two or three weeks, he reaches up to his shelves for a variety of remedies, which he then carefully labels with little scraps of vellum. Bottles are secured with string and sealed. When exhausted by his labours at the workbench, Cadfael can take his rest among the soft rugs on a long seat opposite, or, on warm days, on the wooden seat outside the door. It is his refuge within a refuge, and very necessary for his peace of mind.

Contemporary readers are becoming increasingly interested in the kind of herbal remedies that Cadfael prepares. For many people natural compounds now appear to be much more attractive than the chemical products of international laboratories. The value of chemicals found in plants is still undervalued but not the least of Cadfael's wide appeal is his understanding of medicinal plants. Ellis Peters has researched the topic thoroughly and admits to still having a great deal to learn, but seven years spent in a chemist's shop before the war gave her a good basic knowledge of drugs and their uses. In those days the village pharmacist was likely to make up many of the medicines that he dispensed so his assistant would have been familiar with many potent compounds. She knew the plant provenance of most drugs at the time and this background acquired from practical experience has been augmented since with books such as *Culpeper's Illustrated Herbal*, John Harvey's *Medieval Gardens*, and Tony Hart's *Plant Names of Medieval England*. Peters's careful scholarship has been recognised by experts in the field, and a recent article in *The Pharmaceutical Journal* gives extensive coverage of the plants that Cadfael cultivated for his remedies.

Contrary to general expectation, Ellis Peters has never been a fanatical gardener, and while her brother was alive she was quite happy to leave this domain to him. Now she enjoys her roses in a relatively labour-free garden and leaves the more strenuous work to Cadfael and his apprentices, in the world of the imagination.

Inevitably, in coming to a conclusion about the Chronicles of Brother Cadfael, the thoughtful reader is bound to reflect on the nature of Cadfael's faith, and on the beliefs of his creator. Peters has said of Brother Cadfael, 'He has underlined my belief. I have to say I am a religious person. I don't go to church because I do not feel the need. I would like to attend more often but often I find church services irrelevant and disappointing.' Yet Peters gave readings in Shrewsbury Abbey as part of the nine hundredth anniversary celebrations and she takes a great interest in plans for the restoration of the building and its surroundings. Her Christianity, like Cadfael's, seems to be firmly rooted in its social structures rather than its dogma. On the question of miracles she admits to holding an open mind:

> I agree with Brother John, who feels that one can derive comfort and help from a saint without wanting to possess her bones; tangible relics seem irrelevant. Faith is another matter. Faith and grace, a pretty powerful mixture... Physical relics seem to me unnecessary, but there are places where centuries

of faith have accumulated, as it were, an ambience in which miracles seem perfectly possible. Saint Winifred's Well, for one.

The nature of Cadfael's faith has been well examined by Mary McDermott Shideler in her essay 'The Whodunnit is Fiction's Most Moral Genre' in the American publication *Books and Religion* where she concludes that 'Cadfael's is an earthly holiness; there is little that he does not know by observation and experience of love and hate, loyalty and betrayal, intelligence and stupidity, the serenity of cloister and the travail of battle.' Similarly, Father John Harriott, writing in the international Catholic weekly *The Tablet* on 11 October 1986, recognises the conjunction of faith and humanity in these novels:

> But most powerful of all is the sense of a society in which the natural and supernatural march easily together, and of a moral order which is not artificially imposed but the very climate in which men live and breathe and have their being. It is this that Cadfael understands and interprets with such insight that he is more than a detective bringing the guilty to book but rather a healer of wounded psyches, concerned less with retribution than redemption. Finally, there is the picture of a structured monastic life where prayer, work, recreation, study all have their place, each monk knows his duties and possesses a sense of worth. (p.1066)

Or, as Ellis Peters herself puts it, in rather simpler terms, the books are liked by her readers because 'they offer a degree of hope and consolation, and leave people feeling better, not worse about their fellow creatures and their situation in this imperfect world.' The following chapter explores the varied world of Brother Cadfael in twenty novels and three short stories spanning the years 1137 to 1145. In less than seventeen years, since the first chronicle in 1977, Ellis Peters has created not just a series of novels, but a significant fictional world.

7. The Chronicles of Brother Cadfael

Tracks of ancient occupation. Frail ironworks rusting in the
  thorn-thicket. Hearthstones; charred lullabies. A solitary
  axe-blow that is the echo of a lost sound.

Tumult recedes as though into the long rain. Groves
  of legendary holly; silverdark the ridged gleam.
  Mercian Hymns by Geoffrey Hill

Possession of a saint, in medieval Europe, represented both economic advantage and spiritual power. According to R.H.C. Davis, writing in his book *A History of Medieval Europe*:

> Medieval people had difficulty in distinguishing between the concrete and the abstract. The moment they saw holiness, they wanted to possess it. They collected holy men and women as a Renaissance prince collected artists, or as a scholar collects books and calls it 'learning'. Their aim was not to subscribe to a Central Fund for the Promotion of Monasticism, nor to further missionary work in distant parts. They wanted holy monks to come and live near them on their own lands. (pp.253-54)

Professor Davis sees holiness as a formidable social force: 'Men would travel hundreds of miles to pray at the tomb of a saint; they would pay vast sums of money even for a small relic, for then the saint might intercede for the soul of the guilty suppliant.'

A Morbid Taste for Bones, the first Cadfael novel, published in 1977, explores the issue thoroughly. Historical records show that the Prior of Shrewsbury Abbey, Prior Robert Pennant, led a group of monks to the village of Gwytherin in North Wales in 1137 to plead for the bones of St Winifred, who was known to be buried there. He secured the bones and brought them back to the abbey where they were enshrined and became a focal point for pilgrimage. These are the facts as far as they are known. To them Ellis Peters brought a rich and often dryly amusing narrative about the expedition and the personalities of the people involved. She invents two murders and supplies a romance. There is a beautiful heroine who is rescued from danger just in time. Much is learned about the distinctive social order of the Welsh; their laws, their ancient Celtic Christianity and such curious customs as the absence of money in the organisation of their affairs. When Prior Robert offers money for the saint, he could not have been guilty of a more powerful insult. The author's sympathies are clearly on the Welsh, not the Norman, side of Offa's Dyke.

Cadfael enters the first novel as an outsider on the inside and he maintains that position throughout the series. He is an outsider because he is Welsh and he sides with his fellow countrymen who are quite happy to keep their little saint where she is, even though the grave is somewhat neglected. He is an insider because he has sworn his oath of obedience to the Benedictine Order and must do what he is told. The routes to this obedience become more and more convoluted, yet none of his later schemes begin to compare in sheer audacity to the one in this book, where another corpse is substituted for the remains of the saint in order to shield a young man who is unjustly accused of murder. When the monks have returned to Shrewsbury, reverently seen on their way by the entire village of Gwytherin, all of them well-apprised, but silent, about the fact that their saint remains where she always was, Cadfael is relieved that the mission has been satisfactorily completed. As he dozes behind his pillar in the chapter house he feels reasonably content: 'Letting the devout voices slip out of his consciousness, Cadfael congratulated himself on having made as many people as possible happy'. There is no doubt whatsoever that making people happy is always going to be more important to Cadfael than abstract devotions, although he does wrestle occasionally with his conscience as crowds of pilgrims arrive to seek blessing from the reliquary in St Winifred's Chapel.

He finally confesses to Hugh Beringar four years later in *The Pilgrim of Hate*:

> 'From the moment I raised her,' said Cadfael, 'and, by God, it was I who took her from the soil, and I who restored her—

and still that makes me glad — from the moment I uncovered those slender bones, I felt in mine they wished only to be left in peace. It was so little and so wild and quiet a graveyard there, with the small church long out of use, meadow flowers growing over all, and the mounds so modest and green. And Welsh soil! The girl was Welsh, like me, her church was of the old persuasion, what did she know of this alien English shire? And I had those young things to keep. Who would have taken their word or mine against all the force of the church? They would have closed their ranks to bury the scandal, and bury the boy with it, and he guilty of nothing but defending his dear. So I took measures.' (pp.16-17)

The establishment of Cadfael's secret in the first novel of the series gives the reader an intimate relationship with the central character. Like all loveable rogues he breaks the rules in order to help others, while seeking nothing for himself. Peters was reinventing a classic anti-hero figure in Brother Cadfael even though the exterior might appear to be distinctly unpromising. The dramatic irony set up between Cadfael, the reader and the more orthodox members of the abbey, such as Prior Robert, creates a pleasing sense of engagement with the past, and invites the reader again and again to side with the abbey's outsider, the person who still manages to achieve St Winifred's grace while breaking all the rules.

One Corpse Too Many (1979) follows the historical records closely. It brings into the novel much more of the civil war that was to tear England apart for several years, based on the quarrel over who was to succeed King Henry I as King of England. Having lost his only lawful son in a shipwreck Henry had made his barons swear loyalty to his daughter, the Empress Matilda (sometimes called Maud). Meanwhile his nephew Stephen, aided by his brother, Henry of Blois, rushed to claim the throne. From then on, alliances developed and declined, loyalties were tested, towns were destroyed and many innocent citizens perished.

Shrewsbury Castle and town were held by the powerful Sheriff William FitzAlan, who supported the empress. This placed the abbey in a difficult position, as their support leaned in the opposite direction, even though they tried to stay aloof from the fighting. In the summer of 1138 King Stephen determined to take the town, and beseiged the castle and the town walls for four days, doing considerable damage. When Stephen's forces eventually broke through the defences, the king, in an unusual burst of savage decisiveness, ordered all ninety-four defenders to be hanged from the castle walls. At this point history ends and the novel begins.

Ninety-four corpses means ninety-four burials, and the monks of the Abbey feel it their duty to assist. Cadfael is known to have fought in battle and handled many dead. Abbot Heribert asks him to take charge of the burials, and with a heavy heart he agrees to do so. Only when the corpses have been laid out ready for burial does the weary Cadfael walk down the long row and count the bodies. There is one too many. It does not take long for him to find one whose death came by efficient strangling, not the crude hangman's noose.

The novel gains considerable stature from the gravity of this scene, and the memory of corpses hanging from the castle walls. Citizens of Shrewsbury recover the dead that they know and bury them themselves. The rest of the troops are buried in a mass grave in the abbey grounds specially consecrated by the abbot. In our days of mass destruction ninety-five dead does not appear to be a vast number, yet Peters carefully builds up the horror and the sadness at this tragedy for a small town. When a country is split by warring factions many of the innocent suffer and Cadfael finds himself involved in rescuing Godith, the daughter of one of the rebel leaders, Fulke Adeney, and sending her off with FitzAlan's treasure.

This is the novel which introduces us to Hugh Beringar, and his dark sardonic presence causes Cadfael a great deal of disquiet. Although Hugh has pledged allegiance to Stephen's party he is known to be connected to FitzAlan and so is not completely trusted by either side. He and Cadfael stalk each other throughout the unsettled days of the seige and its aftermath, and Cadfael's attendance at services becomes a little erratic as he hurries around the fugitives that he has hidden in or near the abbey before managing to get them away, with the treasure, to the Welsh coast and a boat to France. Cadfael's deception of Beringar and the younger man's good-humoured acceptance of a battle of wits fairly played and lost establishes their long-lasting friendship.

Appropriately for a tale that involves kings, castles, seiges and hidden treasure, *One Corpse Too Many* ends with knightly combat. Hugh Beringar proves himself before King Stephen by challenging one of his officers, Adam Courcelle, to a duel, having accused him of murdering the mysterious stranger. The duel takes place in a meadow beyond the Castle Foregate, where the river twists and turns across green turf. Peters revels in her description of the colour and the drama of the scene:

> The slanting light of morning cast long but delicate shadows across the grass, and the sky above was thinly veiled with haze. Cadfael lingered where guards held a path clear for the procession approaching from the castle, a brightness of steel and sheen of gay colours bursting suddenly out of the dim archway of the gate. King Stephen, big, flaxen-haired, handsome, resigned now to the necessity that threatened to rob him of one of his officers, but none the better pleased for that, and not disposed to allow any concessions that would prolong the contest. (p.353)

Cadfael, who is by now convinced of Beringar's worth, asks for permission to attend him, and as swords are unsheathed he forgets his role as man of the cloth 'and doubted that all these tranquil years since he took the cowl had really made any transformation in a spirit once turbulent, insubordinate and incorrigibly rash. He could feel his blood rising, as though it was he who must enter the lists.' Although Cadfael has seen enough of the world to know that good men do not always triumph and that God's will is not always revealed in the way we think best, he nevertheless is very satisfied with the unexpected outcome, when Adam Courcelle falls on his own poniard and Beringar is innocent of his death. Beringar is appointed deputy sheriff and his place as the king's servant is secure. Yet typically, as he and Cadfael discuss the mysteries that they have resolved together, they share a philosophical view of justice that allows for a wider sweep than that of Stephen or Maud. Cadfael concludes that 'God disposes all. From the highest to the lowest extreme of a man's scope, wherever justice and retribution can reach him, so can grace.' Many of the mysteries which follow allow for divine retribution rather than that of the state. Beringar knows to busy himself elsewhere when Cadfael is at work on behalf of those whom he recognises as guilty, but feels sure were never meant to be murderers. It is a curious category but allows for what one might call natural justice in a state where property often seems to be more important than human lives. Such a criminal appears in her next novel, *Monk's-Hood*.

Despite Peters's knowledge of poisons and their effects, few of the Chronicles actually see murder done by lethal dose. *Monk's-Hood*

(1980) deals with murder by poison, and to Cadfael's great distress, the poison is of his own distillation, stolen from a vial that he left in the infirmary to be used as a liniment for the aches and pains of elderly monks. Monk's-Hood is a tall, showy, violet-flowered plant that has been known from ancient times as having both healing and destructive properties. It is still used in homeopathic medicines today, where it is valued as an ingredient in ointments for aching joints. The most poisonous part of the plant is the tuberous root, which resembles a turnip, and Cadfael is quite correct when he says that even a tiny quantity is enough to kill a man. He is meticulous in wiping the rim of his large container in the shed and warns Brother Edmund to be sure to wash his hands carefully after using the salve. Cadfael has added mustard and other herbs to this rub so that it is very aromatic, and the powerful and long-lasting odour is used by Cadfael to trap the murderer. The events surrounding this puzzling event take place in the winter of 1138. The town of Shrewsbury is still trying to re-establish itself after King Stephen's seige earlier in the year, and there is general relief that the civil war between the king and the empress was being fought at a distance. Preparations are being made to celebrate Christmas at the abbey and Cadfael is busy in his workshop brewing various medicaments for use in the winter months ahead. Newly established in a house within the abbey grounds is the wealthy landowner Gervase Bonel and his wife Richildis, who has undertaken to give his border manor to the Benedictines in exchange for food and care for the rest of their lives. Before the documents can be signed, however, Bonel is poisoned. Suspicion immediately falls on Edwin, his stepson, who had hoped to inherit the manor, and who had quarrelled often with his imperious relation. But Cadfael soon discovers that others besides Edwin could bear a grudge against Bonel, including his natural son Meurig and a disaffected servant, Aelfric. Cadfael is particularly anxious to help clear Edwin's name when he discovers that his mother, Richildis, is his first love whom he abandoned when he went off to the Crusades. A cosy evening chat between them ends up with Cadfael accused of impropriety by Brother Jerome and banned from leaving the abbey precinct; highly inconvenient for a busy sleuth with many leads to follow up. Cadfael's assistant Brother Mark proves his worth here and not only reveals surprising skills at hurling pebbles but manages to find the incriminating empty vial of poison that Cadfael had been seeking.

Peters introduces several interesting examples of monastic and legal organisation at that time, particularly the differences between Welsh and English law. Illegitimacy is not taken as a bar to inheriting property under Welsh law and the desperate attempt by Meurig to claim the land where he grew up and the manor that he loves is well understood by Brother Cadfael. Meurig's unaccountable escape westwards into Wales on a horse belonging to the abbey (through the carelessness of Brother Cadfael, who left the stable door un-barred) allows for a peaceful and simple Christmas with the shep-herds on the Welsh mountains: 'It was a good Christmas: he had never known one more firelit and serene. The simple outdoor labour was bliss after stress, he would not have exchanged it for the cere-monial and comparative luxury of the abbey.'

Peters's growing confidence in her fictional world and in the materials that she had on hand in local archives led her to write three novels which can certainly be regarded as the best of the series: *St Peter's Fair* (1981), *The Leper of St Giles* (1981) and *The Virgin in the Ice* (1982). All are rich in detail, well characterised and inventively plotted, sharing a freshness of vision that is sometimes, perhaps inevitably in a series of this length, lacking in later books.

St Peter's Fair is the novel which depicts more clearly than any of the others the colour and quality of life in the town of Shrewsbury. Most towns of any size would have hosted a summer fair for Lammas Tide, the first three days of August. It was also a religious feast to do with the harvest festival, and was known as the Loaf Mass. In Shrewsbury the fair took its name from the Saint's Day of St Peter, one of the patron saints of the abbey.

The fair is an important source of income for the abbey and Abbot Radulfus, newly installed in place of Abbot Heribert, initially refuses the request from the tradesmen to deviate from the king's charter and allow part of the profits to be granted towards repairing the damaged streets and walls of the town. The delegation of the chief tradesmen, led by the provost, master shoemaker Geoffrey Corviser, stalk away from chapter disappointed but dignified. Their disap-pointment, but not their dignity, is taken over by their sons and leads to confrontation with visiting merchants who are unloading their goods along the banks of the Severn near the Abbey Foregate where the fair is held. Ultimately there is a riot along the jetty with bales and barrels being tossed into the river and most of the promising youth of the town being flung into jail. The provost's son, Philip

Corviser, is ring-leader of the group.

The fair carries on successfully and Peters gives a vivid sense of the rich merchants in their stalls, with rare goods imported from the East, the pedlars with their packs of ribbons and coloured cloths, and the country people with their produce, together with all the crowds who have come to buy and to enjoy each other's holiday company. Such a scene is entertaining and enjoyable, but we are soon reminded that this is a time of conspiracy and treason. A meeting place such as St Peter's Fair is a ideal place for clandestine messages to be exchanged and for spies from both factions of the civil war to note any suspicious encounters. The sheriff and his deputy and, it must be admitted, Brother Cadfael, are slow to pick up the political implications of the murder of Robert of Bristol, the ransacking of his barge and the theft of his strongbox. Not until Robert's handsome niece Emma has innocently ridden away with her uncle's murderer does the intrigue become clear, and this is the chance for the disgraced Philip Corviser to show his qualities. Emma, too, has behaved heroically by thrusting her hand into a burning brazier to ensure that the secret letter she carried would catch well alight and be impossible to retrieve.

In a tale which celebrates the mercantile virtues of the town it is not surprising that Emma, who is well aware of her own eligibility, realises very quickly that she has no desire to leave the solid burgher comforts and the sober values of her own merchant class. Philip's headlong dash to save Emma gives a stirring finish to the novel and proves that even a shoemaker's son can act with valour. His courtship seems set to prosper. The fair over, Abbot Radulfus allows a donation to be made to repair the town and honour is maintained on all sides. As the Welsh merchant Master Rhodri remarks to Cadfael, 'both halves of England can meet in commerce, while they fall out in every other field. Show a man where there's money to be made, and he'll be there. If barons and kings had the same good sense, a country could be at peace, and handsomely the gainer by it.'

In *The Leper of St Giles* Peters brings romance very much to the centre of the narrative. We know from the opening pages that when young Iveta, being brought unwillingly to a marriage in the abbey, throws alms to the waiting crowd of lepers outside St Giles and smiles at them, she will be cherished by Cadfael, and so she is. Her bridegroom, who had ridden down the highroad before her, had whipped the lepers and sworn at their presence; a bad sign and so it proves.

Leprosy is a disease now associated only with tropical climates yet in the Middle Ages it was widespread throughout Europe. It is likely that it was spread by Crusaders returning from the East. There was no cure, and lepers were condemned to wander, seeking what alms they could while staying away from any centres of population. Among the duties of the Benedictine Order was the care and healing of the sick, and the abbey of St Peter and St Paul maintained a small hospice or lazar house at the church of St Giles, a short distance from the abbey along the Foregate. The church was built in the early twelfth century and still stands today, although it was heavily altered in the nineteenth century. The hospital, in its wattle enclosure, has completely disappeared.

Cadfael visits the lepers every two or three weeks to tend their sores and to replenish the medicine cupboard. From his scrip he unpacks 'jars of salves and bottles of lotion made from alkanet, anemone, mint, figwort and the grains of oat and barley, most of them herbs of Venus and the moon.' He also has fierce plasters of mustard for malignant sores. His former helper and great favourite Brother Mark is in charge of the sick at St Giles, and Mark is eventually replaced by Brother Oswin when he goes to become a priest.

Although Abbot Radulfus accepts that powerful marriages are often arranged with more concern to consolidate property than to benefit bride or groom, he shares Cadfael's uneasiness about the marriage arranged for eighteen year old Iveta with a sixty year old man. (The reverse situation is explored in *The Hermit of Eyton Forest* where a young boy is almost forced into marriage with an older girl.) Nevertheless the wedding seems inevitable until Huon de Domville is found lying dead in the forest, strangled. Typically of Peters's plots a young suitor to Iveta is blamed for the crime. He manages to escape from the sheriff's escort by leaping over the bridge into the chilly waters of the river Severn. Ultimately he ends up sheltering at St Giles, wearing the cape and veil of a leper.

His choice of refuge neatly draws together aspects of the plot which only Cadfael is able to see. Iveta is the granddaughter of the famous crusader Guimar de Massard, with whom Cadfael served at the storming of the gates of Jerusalem. He had always been presumed dead of his wounds although his body was never returned to England. Cadfael is able to deduce that the tall, dignified leper who shelters Joscelin Lucy is in fact de Massard. He has spent the past eight years walking to England from his hermitage in the Middle

East to look after the interests of his granddaughter. Once justice is done, and the girl's uncle has also met summary judgement in the forest, he departs without trace, his ravaged body having still allowed him to fulfill his purpose.

The Virgin in the Ice must surely rank with *The Heaven Tree* trilogy as being among Peters's finest historical fiction. Vivid pictures of southern Shropshire in the grip of the deeply cold December of 1139 are overlaid by the unforgettable image of the title, the murdered nun who is found frozen into the waters of a shallow brook.The narrative is complex and full of interest, with several intricate strands weaving the plot into a richly textured tapestry. Civil war has reached Worcester and among the refugees from the sacked city are two young people who have been in the care of the Benedictines, thirteen year old Yves Hugonin and his sister Ermina, who is nearly eighteen. With them on their flight towards Shrewsbury is a young nun, Sister Hilaria, who had been Ermina's tutor. The party has disappeared without trace.

Cadfael is brought into the southern part of the county by a request for his skills from the Prior of Bromfield. Bromfield is twenty miles from Shrewsbury and it is a difficult journey in severe conditions. Snow is heavy on the ground and more is falling as Cadfael makes his lonely way to help restore a monk who had been attacked and left for dead by the roadside. As he listens to the injured man's delirious words, Cadfael realises that he is hearing part of the story of the fate of the Hugonin children. He sets off next day to make enquiries in the bleak landscape of Clee forest. Not only does he find Yves, who is safe in a forester's hut, he also finds Sister Hilaria as he crosses a frozen stream:

> Out of the encasing, glassy stillness a pale, pearly oval stared up at him with open eyes. Small, delicate hands had floated briefly before the frost took hold, and hovered open at her sides, a little upraised as if in appeal. The white of her body and the white of her torn shift which was all she wore seemed to Cadfael to be smirched by some soiling colour at the breast, but so faintly that too intent staring caused the mark to shift and fade. The face was fragile, delicate, young. (p.411)

Violence is everywhere as evidence soon emerges that ruthless raiding parties from the hills have been burning isolated farms, killing all who try to defend their goods and driving away the livestock. Peters brilliantly evokes an atmosphere where intense cold and hard-riding horsemen appear to engulf the few points of warmth and civilisation that still exist. The climax to the novel takes place on the highest hills of the county, the Clee Hills, which rise to almost 1,800 feet. Cadfael tracks the outlaws to a hidden camp on the summit of Titterstone Clee which, although only five miles from Ludlow, is still a bleak and lonely spot, especially in winter. Although the raiders' band is destroyed, Cadfael knows that not every violent crime can be laid to their charge and Sister Hilaria's death calls someone else to account.

Cadfael returns to Shrewsbury Abbey in time for the Christmas feast, and shares the happiness of Hugh and Aline Beringar at the birth of their son Giles. While Hugh exults in the birth of his child, Cadfael, too, has experienced unexpected joy in meeting Olivier de Bretagne who is sent to escort the Hugonin children to their uncle, just returned from the Crusades. Olivier confides to Cadfael that he is the son of Mariam, a widow of Antioch and an English soldier and he tells Cadfael that 'she was beautiful and loving, and he was brave and kind, and I think myself well mothered and fathered, and the equal of any man living.' For Cadfael it is a revelation that he has a worthy son and a blessing for Christmas — 'a time of births, of triumphant begettings.' He also has a new role to play as godfather to Giles, a relationship that brings him much reward in the years ahead.

The Virgin in the Ice remains inventive to the end although the narrative is dominated by the haunting image of the frozen nun, 'a girl in a mirror, a girl spun from glass.' Destructive forces are defeated for the time being but the battle is plainly only one of a series. Cadfael knows that the enduring nature of individual evil will continue to direct many aspects of human society. Fortunately he knows too that the potential for good also exists among rich and poor alike, no matter how far they are tested.

Although the Chronicles of Brother Cadfael continued to emerge almost annually during the 1980s it is fair to say that not all novels reached the high standard of *The Virgin in the Ice* or *The Leper of St Giles*. Peters develops each novel differently to some extent but a recurrent strand in nearly every plot is the trial of young lovers, some privileged and wealthy, some very poor, whose happiness is threatened but who are rescued by the clear-sightedness and ingenuity of Brother Cadfael. (Readers are divided on the appeal of these love affairs. Peters maintains that readers now expect them and miss this aspect of her fiction if not provided; critics have referred to them as 'twee little romances' and have complained about detection being crowded out.) More univerally acceptable is the provision of interesting information about certain aspects of medieval life, particularly life among the craftsmen of the city. Peters takes her researches into the civic background very seriously and told June E. Prance that 'I almost feel that I'm building up a picture of medieval Shrewsbury, with the craftsmen and the merchants and weavers, and the fullers and dyers...and that I've made it a real community. I want to go on doing this. Part of my life is indeed involved in Cadfael's community and I hope I've succeeded in passing this along to the readers.' (p.15) This aspect of local history is reliably documented in Shrewsbury and Peters's use of this material is sound. What is remarkable is the way that she is able to give us the genuine feel of life in a medieval town without, perhaps, indulging overmuch in the mud and smells. Peters claims to adopt the viewpoint of people living in her twelfth-century world, saying in an interview with Mike Ashley that:

> I have read books that emphasize the ugliness and the squalor and the cruelty and the brutality. I think that human nature has been very much the same, equally bad and equally good throughout. People tend to look from a twentieth century viewpoint at the twelfth and thirteenth centuries and think how dreadful it must have been living in such conditions, without recalling that people who did live in those conditions really didn't think much about them. I've tried to write the books from the viewpoint of someone who was there and found all these things quite normal.

The art of using historical material is of course to present it so naturally that the reader does not feel part of an artifical exercise, and Peters is highly successful in achieving this.

Inevitably, as the list of Chronicles grew longer, familiar patterns began to develop. Repetitions in descriptions (such as Hugh's raw-boned grey horse) and even in vocabulary had crept in. This is often unavoidable in a series of novels where the author needs always to provide the basic material necessary for a new reader to derive immediate enjoyment from a situation that is already very familiar to someone who has read all the previous books. Peters's adroit narrative skills manage to bring about this sleight of hand with welcome economy. The balance between the novel and the mystery can be difficult to maintain and the historical and religious dimensions of the Cadfael Chronicles provide additional complications. Sustaining a sense of mystery is not easy when the attraction of character dilutes the intellectual rigour of solving crimes, and recurrent plot devices such as the final confrontation in the abbey courtyard can sometimes round stories off too compactly. Yet Peters possesses a rare ability to continue peopling her world with well-established and richly-detailed characters, whose faces, clothes, hair, speech and demeanour are effortlessly described. Above all, she has given her readers an enduring central character who manages to be both good and humorous; morally sound without being sanctimonious, and full of a true sense of human worth.

The Sanctuary Sparrow (1983) displays some of the problems discussed above yet its positive features outweigh any of its weaknesses. This novel introduces one of Peters's most attractive characters, Liliwin, the jongleur. Liliwin is hunted violently through the streets of the town and into the abbey by an armed mob, having been accused of murder and robbery. Abbot Radulfus grants him sanctuary for forty days as custom demands. Claims for sanctuary from the law were taken seriously in the Middle Ages and many cathedrals or abbeys kept special watch for desperate fugitives who might urgently need admission. (The famous sanctuary knocker on the door of Durham Cathedral had only to be grasped by a person in flight to secure help.)

Although the novel opens dramatically with Liliwin noisily disrupting the midnight service of Matins in the abbey, it soon settles down into the investigation of a robbery and subsequently a murder. More abstractly it is a study of avarice; as Madog the boatman says of Dame Juliana, head of the wealthy Aurifaber family, 'Avarice is a destroying thing, Cadfael, and she bred them all in her own shape, all get and precious little give.' The household of the goldsmith Walter Aurifaber seems to be dogged by misfortune: robbery, assault and murder. Over it presides Dame Juliana, whose iron will has, up to now, controlled them all. The story ends on a strong moral tone as two mature lovers , one of whom is Juliana's granddaughter, spend too long collecting their stolen wealth and are trapped by their greed.

In contrast, Liliwin and the Aurifaber's servant Rannilt, who have no possessions between them, share a mutual affection that sees them married at the same altar where Liliwin flung himself down pleading for sanctuary at the beginning of the story. Even Liliwin's damaged rebec has been carefully reconstructed and forty days with Brother Anselm has given him the opportunity to learn to read music and play the organetto. Brother Anselm has also gained, having written down a number of Liliwin's ballads for future refurbishment as religious motifs. The town burghers, guilty at the hue and cry which could easily have led to Liliwin's death, send useful gifts of shoes and clothing to see him and Rannilt on their way. But if *The Sanctuary Sparrow* has a sweet note in relation to Liliwin and Rannilt it also has a dour refrain that accompanies the grasping tyranny of wealth and the equation of human relationships with money and goods. 'I would have taken her barefoot in her shift', cries Susanna's lover, but she would not go without gold and she loses not only her own life but the life of her unborn child. Although Hugh is horrified by Susanna's ruthlessness Cadfael, as we would expect, is more charitable and feels that her upbringing had much to do with her corrupted end.

The civil war haunts all the novels but has more prominence in some than in others. In *The Devil's Novice* (1983) the political conspiracy does not emerge until the very end, and the central moral problem which holds the reader is the conflict between father and son. Through the character of nineteen year old Meriet Aspley the novel also touches upon the choice made by those who join the order and the personal qualities they require. Meriet's desperation to take his vows quickly makes the abbot suspicious of his motives and eventually he becomes as reluctant to accept Meriet as he was to accept the infant child or oblate offered to the order by a local family. All the young people involved in the tale acquire self-knowledge; Cadfael sees 'the boy become a man and the girl become what she had always been in the bud, a formidable woman.'

Advancing from the clear-cut thrust of youthful judgements to the complexities of adult responsibilities is also a central part of *Dead Man's Ransom*. The ninth chronicle of Brother Cadfael, *Dead Man's Ransom* (1984) ranges up and down the Welsh border from southwest of Shrewsbury to Oswestry. Gilbert Prestcote, the Sheriff of Shrewsbury, has been taken prisoner by Welsh troops while fighting for the king at Lincoln. Hugh Beringar seeks to ransom him with a young Welsh warrior captured rather ignominiously during a raid on the nuns of the Benedictine cell at Godric's Ford. Had Cadwaladr's men known that they would be confronted by the formidable Avice of Thornbury (now known as Sister Magdalen) they might have thought twice about their venture. With three Welsh dead, several wounded and a valuable prisoner, Avice could well present herself to Abbot Radulfus with considerable satisfaction. Cadfael is delighted to see her again; it is two years since he came to talk to her about the death of Huon de Domville and she took the veil after spending many years as Domville's mistress.

Owain, Prince of Gwynnedd, also appears again in this novel when Cadfael is sent into Wales to negotiate an exchange of hostages. The success of the mission is marred only by the unthinkable happening; the murder of Prestcote in the infirmary of the abbey itself. While Cadfael is pushing his crude forensic skills to the utmost in solving the murder he is also much exercised in unpicking the romantic entanglements of four young people.

Dead Man's Ransom provides an exploration of a relationship between two foster-brothers that is so close it leads to murder. The novel also reveals how the two couples mature during the moral testing that confronts them all. It is ironic that the harsh dispenser of justice Gilbert Prestcote has no one to answer for his murder; he himself had been swift to judge while he held the law in Shropshire.

The theme of revenge lies at the heart of *The Pilgrim of Hate* (1984). A murder in the court of Bishop Henry of Winchester is eventually resolved along the Roman road near the castle of Caus on the Welsh border. Here the opportunity for an avowed revenge is offered to young Luc Meverel, and he passes it by, having learned, as he later tells Abbot Radulfus, 'that in God's hands vengeance is safe. However long delayed, however strangely manipulated, the reckoning is sure.' Other powerful themes are part of the structure of the novel, predominantly the role of faith. The events described are all involved with the fourth anniversary of the arrival of St Winifred's reliquary at the Abbey of St Peter and St Paul. A procession from the church of St Giles to the abbey recreates the original journey and allows the townspeople and many visiting pilgrims to follow the saint to her chapel in the Abbey.

For Cadfael, as one of the bearers of the coffin, the ceremony creates some difficulties. He knows that St Winifred is safely buried where she always was in Wales and he feels guilty that many of the sick are, through faith, hoping for a cure. Cadfael himself would be happy for a small sign of her favour, because although he still feels that he acted for the best, he worries about the amount of power that can emerge from the bones of a sinner, not a saint. The miracle comes to a most worthy recipient, a fifteen year old boy whose leg is crippled and who leaves his crutches at the altar steps. When Cadfael later gives thanks to St Winifred in solitary meditation he senses her care for him as well as for her pilgrims. He takes as a blessing his meeting again with Olivier, his son, who is now married to Ermina Hugonin and who continues in the service of the Empress Maud. The empress is on the brink of being crowned queen in London but so annoys the powerful citizenry that they rise together and drive her away. Far to the west, in Shrewsbury, faith, vengeance and love arrive at peaceful resolution during the few days in June when St Winifred is particularly celebrated. Cadfael's friendship with Hugh is made even firmer by his confession as to the saint's real burial place and also by telling him that Olivier is his son.

The positive themes of *The Pilgrim of Hate* carry over into the next novel, *An Excellent Mystery* (1985). In this book Peters examines with great subtlety the notion of love as faithful service. (The title is taken from the Marriage Ceremony in *The Book of Common Prayer*.) There are no young lovers here, struggling against the odds, but a deeply moving story of a wounded crusader turned monk, Brother Humilis, and his devoted helper, Brother Fidelis. The darker side of love and desire manifests itself in the bitterness of Brother Urien who imposes himself on Brother Rhun and Brother Fidelis as he wrestles with his sexual longings.

Like all Peters's most satisfying novels in the Cadfael series, the novel has a number of intertwining strands. The steady movement of the old Crusader towards his death, despite Cadfael's best efforts to heal his wound, has as its counterpoint the increasingly desperate search by his former squire to find the missing woman Julian Cruce. Incriminating evidence accumulates against a servant of the family but thanks to hasty and determined action by Cadfael and his old friend Sister Magdalen the young woman who had been feared dead is brought back to life:

> The burial of Brother Humilis had become in a moment the resurrection of Julian Cruce, from a mourning into a celebration, from Good Friday to Easter. 'A life taken from us and a life restored,' said Abbot Radulfus, 'is perfect balance, that we may fear neither living nor dying.' (p.241)

Even Urien's torment is assuaged by the secret knowledge that he and Brother Rhun share between them. *An Excellent Mystery* ends with an enduring belief in love as a powerful force for good whose effects go far beyond individual relationships. For once the loose ends are not tidied away and while no real crime is committed in the whole novel there is still a very profound sense of the qualities of good and evil, in the abstract and the real.

'Sinners are in your province, not mine,' says Hugh Beringar to Abbot Radulfus at the end of *The Raven in the Foregate* (1986). It is a novel which continues Peters's examination of serious themes by looking at the question of moral responsibility and guilt — guilt which is shared in this case by the abbot himself. He brings Father Ailnoth to be parish priest of the Holy Cross, in the Abbey Foregate. In fact the church of this parish is the nave of the abbey and old Father Adam, who has just died, has held a long and humane tenure among the townspeople who live there. Like his verger, Cynric, he 'would not send you empty away' and is regarded by Prior Robert and Brother Jerome to have been far too forgiving to the sinners in his parish.

Father Ailnoth turns out to be a very different shepherd to his flock and within weeks he has alienated almost everyone because of his harsh attitudes. This includes beating children who play near his house and refusing to leave his prayers to baptize a sick child, who then dies unblessed. When Ailnoth is found floating in the ice-fringed waters of the mill pool, the parish share in a mixture of guilt and satisfaction:

> In the Foregate a kind of breathless hush brooded. People talked much but in low voices and only among trusted friends, and yet everywhere there was a feeling of suppressed and superstitious gladness, as if a great cloud had been lifted from the parish. Even those who did not confide in one another in words did so in silent glances. The relief was everywhere, and palpable.
>
> But so was the fear. For someone, it seemed, had rid the Foregate of its blight, and all those who had wished it away felt a morsel of the guilt sticking to their fingers. (p.104)

Ailnoth meets his chilly end at exactly the same spot where young Eluned drowned herself having been refused confession by him and shut out of the church. For Cynric, who saw the priest fall backwards into the water, it was a judgement. He does nothing to rescue him: 'If God had willed him to live, he would have lived. Why else should it happen there, in that very place? And who am I, to usurp the privilege of God?'

The sheriff does not find any charges to make against the verger but the author has raised yet another moral conundrum for the reader to consider. Should Cynric have tried to rescue a man he hated, a man who fell into the mill pond because he was beating a woman with his staff? And how much responsibility did Abbot Radulfus hold, having introduced this stranger to the parish in the first place, even though it was at the request of the papal legate? *The Raven in the Foregate* deals with the classic conflict between natural justice and the law, with the additional complexity that the man who had beaten the children, left a child to die unbaptized and caused a suicide was a priest. Clearly in the author's view the moral strength in the situation lies with the ordinary people of the Foregate, who help each other in times of difficulty and tolerate each other's weaknesses, rather than with a religious leader who was, in the abbot's description, 'a man with every virtue, except humility and human kindness.'

A sub-plot connects these events to the political struggles of the nation when a young man of FitzAlan's party arrives in Shrewsbury in disguise and has to be shielded by Brother Cadfael until he gets away safely with his young lady. The king's party is again in the ascendant and Stephen is seeking to consolidate his influence. Both the sheriff and the abbot are called to their respective centres of power, Hugh to the king in Canterbury and the abbot to the papal legate in Westminster. Even in these times, when transport was particularly difficult, the centre still kept firm control of its shires.

Peters's next novel, *The Rose Rent* (1986) focuses very closely on the domestic life of Shrewsbury and its citizens. Property and wealth drive the ambitious to unlawful acts, and eventually, to murder. It is also a narrative which considers the position of a young widow who is overburdened with suitors from all sides.

In Chaucer's *Canterbury Tales*, the Wife of Bath is a cheerful, lusty woman who thrives on her four-times widowhood. Each husband leaves her better off than before, so that she can afford to love her fifth young man unreservedly, without any financial limitations. Chaucer is more than sympathetic to this wonderfully zestful character and gives the woman's viewpoint in a convincing and humorous way. Unlike the Wife of Bath, Judith Perle in *The Rose Rent* is oppressed by the attentions she receives. Although she is perfectly capable of managing her business as the chief clothier in the town she finds no pleasure in her work and thinks about taking the veil. Her decision matters, because her business is an important one to the local economy. She provides a living for twenty families in the town, carding, spinning, and weaving the wool on which Shrewsbury's wealth was based. Her property is typical of many of the workshops ranged along the narrow streets of the town:

> The burgage of the Vestier family occupied a prominent place at the head of the street called Maerdol, which led downhill to the western bridge. A right-angled house, with wide shopfront on the street, and the long stem of the hall and chambers running well back behind, with a spacious yard and stables. There was room enough in all that elongated building, besides the living rooms of the family, to house ample stores in a good dry undercroft, and provide space for all the girls who carded and combed the newly dyed wool, beside three horizontal looms set up in their own outbuilding, and plenty of room in the long hall for half a dozen spinsters at once. (p.52)

Judith now lives with her aunt and her cousin above the workshops. The house where she lived during her brief but very happy marriage lies down the hill across the river in the Abbey Foregate. Unable to bear living there after her loss, she has given the house to the abbey for the peppercorn rent of one white rose a year from the rose bush in the garden. Since the income from renting the house is used to light and drape St Winifred's altar all year round, it is appropriate that the rose be delivered on the day of the saint's translation to the abbey, 22 June.

Such a quaint ceremony would appear to be far removed from the prospect of violence, but two deaths emerge from this apparently blameless situation, and the centre of the crimes is the white rose tree. If the tree is destroyed, the rent cannot be paid, the house is lost to the abbey and this valuable property is restored to the widow's already substantial holdings.

The narrative is particularly well supported by detailed descriptions of the town and the river banks. The processes involved in producing woven cloth garments are clearly explained. Where the novel disappoints is in the characterisation of Judith Perle. She remains distant, dignified and strong but a great deal more could be said about this twelfth century businesswoman. Judith is resilient enough to survive kidnapping and a knife attack in the forest and still have enough sangfroid to devise a plan which allows her to escape while not besmirching her abductor. Sister Magdalen's quiet Benedictine cell at Godric's Ford again comes in handy when trying to account for days that form embarrassing gaps in the lives of respectable ladies.

Ultimately the motive for all the disruptions surrounding the Perle household is greed. Judith may be a desirable catch as she stands but she is even more desirable with the valuable property in the Foregate. For once Cadfael and Hugh are completely taken in by the murderer — 'a man may dissemble very well, up to a point, but I never knew a man who could sweat at will', says Hugh confidently but he is quite mistaken in his assessment. Cadfael's close observation of detail and his forensic proof arising from a wax imprint of a footprint eventually trap the murderer, who remains unsuspected to the very end. Judith, like Cadfael, does not see him as evil: '...he found himself where he had never thought or meant to be, in some place he could not even recognise, and not knowing how he made his way there.' Or, as Mary Wollstonecraft observed nearly seven centuries later about the timeless quality of evil, 'No man chooses evil because it is evil; he only mistakes it for happiness, the good he seeks.'

The novel ends on a note of quiet fulfillment for Judith Perle, with her happiness entrusted to an honourable craftsman, a widower, who 'was the one creature about her who had never asked or expected anything, made no demands, sought no advantages, was utterly without greed or vanity, and to him she owed more than merely her life. He had brought her a rose, the last from the old stem, a small miracle.' He also brings, the reader notes with satisfaction, his child Rosalba, another rose for Judith Perle.

Marriage, and its significance in social and political terms, is a theme continued in *The Hermit of Eyton Forest* (1987). Central to the novel is the contentious issue of child marriage; in this case, the attempt by an ambitious grandmother to achieve a profitable alliance in land and property by marrying her ten year old grandson to a twenty-two year old woman who is heir to the neighbouring estate. In contrast to this obsession with property, the story of the runaway villein Brand who freely courts a forester's daughter beneath the oak trees of Eyton Forest seems innocent and romantic. Brand is hunted by the law first for attacking a steward on his master's estate, then as a suspected murderer, but his name is cleared and he and Annet can look forward to making a settled life together with Brand using his skills as a leather worker in Shrewsbury. But there is a third and more complex relationship threading through the narrative, and it is this which sets the train of events in motion and links Shrewsbury with Oxford where the Empress Maud is beseiged. The empress has managed to send jewels and a letter out of Oxford by a trusted messenger, Renaud Bourchier, in an attempt to reach her supporter Brian FitzCount in Wallingford. Her messenger, the letter and the jewels disappear. When Cadfael has finally unravelled the events surrounding this mystery he tells Hugh what has happened:

> 'Only consider, Hugh, her situation when she wrote. The town lost, only the castle left, and the king's armies closing round her. And Brian who had been her right hand, her shield and sword, second only to her brother, separated from her by those few miles that could as well have been an ocean. God knows if those gossips are right,' said Cadfael, 'who declare that those two are lovers, but surely it is truth that they love! And now at this extreme, in peril of starvation, failure, imprisonment, loss, even death, perhaps never to meet again, may she not have cried out to him the last truth, without conceal, things that should not be set down, things no other on earth should ever see? Such a letter might be of immense value to a man without scruples, who had a new career to make, and needed the favour of princes. She has a husband years younger than herself, who has no great love for her, nor she for him, one who would not spare a man to come to her aid this summer. Suppose that some day it should be convenient to Geoffrey to repudiate his older wife, and make a second profitable marriage? In the hands of such as Bourchier her letter, her own hand, might provide him the pretext, and for princes the means can always be found.' (pp.222-23)

This marriage, a marriage of state, has its own particular value. On it can depend the fate of a country, not just the fate of two individuals.

Just as the previous novel provided well-researched information about the woollen trade, *The Hermit of Eyton Forest* also introduces some unusual material in the presence of Cuthred, the hermit.

Cuthred arrives as a stranger to the Abbey of Buildwas, impressively bearing the scallop shell and medal to show that he had made the pilgrimage to the shrine of St James at Compostella. With great respect he is taken in to live in the disused hermitage on the lands of the manor of Eaton. These lands are south of the Wrekin, and border the river Severn as it loops lazily south-eastwards from Shrewsbury. The role of the hermit may seem strange to contemporary readers but there is no doubt that it was taken very seriously in the eleventh and twelfth centuries. As R.H.C. Davis reminds us, 'Many lords gave land and protection to a single hermit; for perchance the hermit might become a saint.' And indeed Brother Cuthred quickly commands respect and devotion, 'for the possession of so devout a hermit brought great lustre to the manor of Eaton'.

How unfortunate for the religious ideal (and the veneration of relics and holy men does not seem to be an aspect of medieval life that sits easily with this author) that Cuthred turns out to be an imposter and a murderer. Worst of all, he has betrayed his mistress, the Empress Maud. This is another novel where judicial murder takes place outside the remit of sheriff or his officers. Brian Fitz-Count's vassal kills Renaud Bourcier in single combat and carries away the jewels and the precious letter. Only Cadfael, who dresses the wounds of this quiet visitor to the abbey guest hall, realises what his mission to Shrewsbury has been. Having allowed him to go on his journey back to Wallingford, Cadfael tells Hugh the real story behind the false hermit Cuthred.

The novel ends on an autumnal note, with Cadfael's thoughts resting on the noble lovers whose situation seems impossible to resolve. Yet two of the tangled relationships with which he has been involved have ended happily; Brand and Annet are looking to the future when Brand will be free of his state as villein, and the reluctant child groom is returned to the care of Abbot Radulfus to finish his education before further thoughts of marriage.

In *The Confession of Brother Haluin* (1988) love is denied its chance to bloom and a labyrinthine mystery is unfolded. The novel begins dramatically later in the winter of 1142-43 when heavy snow falls on Shrewsbury and its surroundings, 'a blinding, silent fall that continued for several days and nights, smoothing out every undulation, blanching all colour out of the world, burying the sheep in the hills and the hovels in the valleys, smothering all sound, climbing every wall, turning roofs into ranges of white, impassable mountains, and he very air between earth and sky into an opaque, drifting whirlpool of flakes large as lilies.' This is the snowfall that envelops the beseiged empress in Oxford Castle and allows her to escape over the frozen river, muffled in white to be invisible in the snow. And it is the same heavy blanket that dislodges the slates on the southern roof of the abbey guest hall, causing damage that must be immediately repaired. The work is cold and dangerous yet every monk takes his turn up on the icy scaffolding. Brother Haluin, the abbey's finest illuminator of manuscripts, works with the rest, and it is he that is lashed off the ladder by an avalanche of snow and sharp-edged slates, falling forty feet to the ground.

Haluin's miraculous survival and the agonised confession that he makes as he lies balanced between life and death opens up another episode in which Brother Cadfael can consider the strange ways of humankind. As soon as Haluin is well enough to hobble on crutches he resolves to go on pilgrimage to the grave of a young girl that he had once loved and now believes to be dead. The burden of her death has lain on his shoulders for nearly twenty years, because messages from her mother claimed that she was with child, and the herbs that Haluin took from Cadfael's store were sent to procure an abortion, and led to her death. That is the truth as Haluin understands it. But as he limps painfully towards Bertrade's grave, with Cadfael as his companion, some mysteries emerge. It is chilly weather in early spring, with frost and snow flurries still taking shelterless wanderers by surprise. The first of two coincidences causes the brothers, driven by a fierce snow storm, to take refuge in an isolated manor where Haluin is asked to perform a hasty marriage. The second, apparently random, call for shelter at the newly-founded convent of Farewell solves the mystery completely, and perhaps strains credulity a little too far. On the other hand, the author is careful to share with the reader Haluin's sense of a path unfolding before him as he seeks God's grace on his personal pilgrimage. He says to Cadfael:

> Nothing is without purpose. How if I fell only to show me how far I was already fallen, and force me to make the assay to rise afresh? How if I came to life again as a cripple, to make me undertake these journeys of body and spirit that I dreaded when I was strong and whole? How if God put it into my mind to go on pilgrimage in order to become some other needy soul's miracle? Were we led to this place? (p.110)

The past despair of Haluin and Bertrade, whose love was cut short, is balanced by a new generation of lovers, Roscelin and Helisende. Only when the hidden truths surrounding Haluin have been confessed can the new relationship flower.

And what about crime? The murder of an elderly woman, nursemaid to the young lovers as children, is incidental to the resolution of the novel, and neither the men who carry it out nor the person who wills it are brought to justice. This is a novel which deals with personal suffering and the hope of salvation, where the past is not allowed to sully the future. For some readers the ending may be too sweet in its cadences; others may find, as in Shakespeare's late romances, that the satisfaction of knowing that wrongs can be set right at last, outweighs any sense of being manipulated by the author.

The Heretic's Apprentice (1989) reveals the author's continuing interest in the spiritual development of her characters, as well as bringing the reader even more closely into the life of the craftsmen of Shrewsbury. This time the mysteries of the vellum-maker are explained in detail, adding an unusual gloss to a well-worked plot. The production of vellum from the skins of sheep or calves was an essential part of the lengthy process that led ultimately to the production of manuscripts of great beauty, decorated with scrupulous and loving care by monks in the scriptoria of religious houses throughout Europe. Great skills were developed in Ireland and spread to Scotland and northern England with the Irish monks who founded communities at Iona and Lindisfarne during the sixth century. Celtic Christianity provided devoted artists and craftsmen whose fine techniques were passed on to religious houses in France, Germany, Italy and Luxemburg as the Irish missionaries, who had kept Christianity alive after the Anglo-Saxon invasions, founded monasteries and brought their scholarship with them. Illuminated gospels and other volumes of scripture were venerated as precious objects and represented substantial investment of time and materials. Powdered gems and gold leaf were used to decorate certain pages, usually initial letters, and many of the manuscripts that have survived, such as the Lindisfarne Gospels or the Book of Kells, still reveal a brightness and lustre that is astonishing so many years after their creation. Even touching such a book was believed to bring healing; to possess one was beyond the dreams of all but the wealthiest nobles. In this novel a beautiful illuminated volume forms temptation that leads to theft and murder, and ultimately to the death of the one who loved books too well.

Readers may be intrigued to know that the production of one book made of vellum could require very large herds of cattle or sheep indeed. The Lindisfarne Gospels is made of one hundred and twenty nine skins, which would have required a breeding herd of nearly seven hundred cows. Only vast estates could afford to sacrifice so many calves for vellum, but in the eighth century the scriptorium at Jarrow, near Durham, managed to produce three volumes at about the same period, each using five hundred calf skins. The production of vellum, therefore, was a major industry, of which the workshop in Shrewsbury was a part.

The ecclesiastical theme is cleverly woven into *The Heretic's Apprentice* by introducing a character who has been on pilgrimage with his master, and comes back to bury his body in the abbey. Young Elave has shared his master's free-thinking views about religion and the conduct of life, and before very long he finds himself locked up in a cell in the abbey on a charge of heresy. Brother Cadfael and Brother Anselm naturally warm to this turbulent soul and provide him with carefully selected texts to read which will help to develop his intellectual grasp of religious belief and also to help prepare for his trial before the bishop. Elave has shocked the more orthodox brethren at the abbey by claiming not to believe in original sin, or to accept that unbaptised infants are damned. Even more alarming, he maintains solidly that salvation is achieved by a man's own acts, not simply by divine grace, and that St Augustine's view that the number of the elect is chosen and cannot be changed is a negation of the individual's right to exercise moral choice. Fortunately for Elave, Bishop Roger de Clinton, who has travelled from Coventry to see him, is more interested in the young man's chiselled-out personal faith than in his supposed heresies, and he is allowed to go free.

The novel has a stirring climax in the vellum workshop on the banks of the Severn which allows Elave to come to the rescue of his young love, Fortunata, ending the novel with the accustomed romantic note. The priceless book, a psalter, which forms the centre-piece to the action, is given to the bishop for his library in Coventry. It has completed a voyage which began in Saint Gallen, with its maker Diarmaid, then continued on first to Byzantium, then to a monastery in Turkey and finally back to England. Appropriately the book which was to be Fortunata's dowry was originally a gift of love, made for the marriage of Otto, Prince of the Roman Empire, to the Princess of Byzantium. Those who search today for the book in Coventry will be disappointed, as this wonderful volume never existed. Peters has said, 'The background account of the Emperor's visit to St Gallen, his son's borrowing of books there, and the young man's marriage to the Princess Theofanu is all true, but the book is imaginary. That's why it could be perfect. I had only to describe it, not produce and show it. Like the church of Parfois in *The Heaven Tree*'.

By the time of the seventeenth novel, *The Potter's Field* (1989), a certain predictability was beginning to affect the novels. In this, however, Peters produces a startlingly unusual and moving tale; one that ranks with her best fictional achievements. The novel centres on the acquisition by the abbey of a well-favoured field sloping down to the banks of the Severn, a field which could profitably be brought into cultivation. It has been exchanged for another property owned by the Augustinian Priory at Haughmond, four miles north-east of Shrewsbury. The transaction provides a reminder that these religious foundations were powerful landowners and careful custodians of their holdings on which the upkeep of the religious houses was based. The pastoral scene of bringing the field under the plough early one morning in October is disrupted when the ploughman brings his straining bullocks rather too close to a clump of broom bushes on the summit of the hill, and dislodges what appears to be a corpse. Although murder, quite reasonably, is suspected when the body of a woman is found, the real explanation is bizarre in the extreme and the reader is kept guessing until the very end of the novel.

The spiritual qualities of the brethren are further examined in this novel, showing Peters's continuing interest in the reasons why religious communities had such appeal during the twelfth century. The character who unknowingly holds responsibility for the crime is also a professed brother who, coming to the cloister after fifteen years of married life and a good while longer plying his craft as a potter, achieves great peace of soul within the order. The question is, at what cost. Aline Beringar, Hugh's wife, normally remains a supportive and silent presence when Hugh and Cadfael talk about their business, but she is unexpectedly judgemental when she gives her opinions about Brother Ruald abandoning his faithful wife Generys:

'Naturally you see the man's rights first, when he sets his heart on doing what he wants, whether its entering the cloister or going off to war, but I'm a woman, and I see how deeply wronged the wife was. Had she no rights in the matter? And did you ever stop to think — *he* could have his freedom to go and become a monk, but his going didn't confer freedom on *her*. She could not take another husband; the one she had, monk or no, was still alive. Was that fair?' (p.10)

And when Cadfael tries to explain to Aline that Ruald seemed almost to have no choice in what he did, in the manner of a saint, Aline replies crisply, 'Is that a saint?... It seems to me all too easy.' Ruald's conduct comes further under scrutiny when he becomes one of the suspects in the investigation of the mysterious corpse found in the Potter's Field.

As in all the best of the Chronicles, unravelling the strands of a local problem leads to wider issues. Hugh and Cadfael begin to focus their attention on the family who own the lands of the manor of Longner, and who had originally owned the Potter's Field. Unexpectedly a younger son of the family, Sulien Blount, a novice at the Abbey of Ramsey, near Huntingdon, arrives at Shrewsbury Abbey with desperate news of the sacking and pillaging of the foundation by Geoffrey de Mandeville, renegade follower of the Empress Maud. Sulien has been sent to deliver news to sister houses, and also sent for a more personal reason, to establish whether he truly wishes to take his vows. Hugh is summoned to provide troops for King Stephen to engage with the rebels and they fight a desultory and inconclusive campaign in the watery marshes of the Fens around Cambridge. Nearly a year after the body has been found in the Potter's Field Hugh and his men return home, mercifully without serious casualties.

Information brought by Hugh from Cambridge closes the ring of suspicion around young Sulien and precipitates the solution of the mystery. Readers who have up to this time felt confident about the conclusion receive a considerable surprise. This is a novel about women and their judgement, and their views are revealed as being very different from those of the men who are involved. Sulien's mother, the Lady Donata, who has for many years suffered in pain from a wasting illness, arrives at the abbey in a litter to tell a bizarre story of two women locked in love for one man. As she finishes her tale, her skin transparent with suffering, Cadfael wonders to himself whether the domain of the church or the law should take precedence: 'Crime was Hugh's business, sin the abbot's, but what was justice here, where the two were woven together so piteously as to be beyond unravelling?'

Those who have sought to protect Donata from the threat to her son have simply undervalued her strength. It has taken 'a conspiracy of women' to work out a solution to the problem, a sharing of truth between the very young and the very old: 'they had come together like lodestone and metal, to compound their own justice'. The novel finishes characteristically with a union between Sulien, who has now left the cloister, and a spirited young woman well matched to his needs. The tone is full of a sombre understanding that leaves the reader stimulated and enlightened by the insights into human nature that have been revealed. The ending to *The Potter's Field* is certainly one of the most gripping pieces of fiction that Peters has ever written.

A long run of novels had now been centered in Shrewsbury and its immediate surroundings. It is not surprising that Peters should seek new territory for her next book, *The Summer of the Danes* (1991), which puts history rather than mystery very much to the foreground. In historical terms, by far the most stirring events of 1144 were happening in Wales, so that is where the author places her protagonists: 'I went where the action was,' says Peters. Cadfael and his much-loved assistant Brother Mark, now in the service of Bishop Roger de Clinton and training to become a priest, make their way across north Wales on an embassy that requires very delicate handling. Their journey from Shrewsbury to deliver a message of support and a gift from the Bishop of Coventry to the newly enthroned Bishop of St Asaph takes them along the same Roman road that Cadfael followed when he was sent to Rhydycroesau to tend a sick brother in *Monk's-Hood*, and Cadfael sniffs the fresh May air with delight. He admits to Brother Mark that 'Shrewsbury is home, and I would not leave it for any place on earth, beyond a visit, but every now and then my feet itch.' The short visit that they plan turns out to be much lengthier and much more dangerous than either might have expected, as the interests of Church and State become inextricably entwined.

Cadfael's occasional forays into Wales allow Peters to introduce material relating to the very different customs existing west of Offa's Dyke. Early in *The Summer of the Danes* the question of celibacy in the clergy arises, because the new Norman Bishop of St Asaph is determined to stamp out the casual practices of the Celtic Church which has allowed priests to marry. Another distinctive aspect of the Celtic Church is the existence of holy wells which bring healing, usually cared for by an anchoress:

> The Church in Wales had never run to nunneries, as even conventual life for men had never been on the same monastic pattern as in England. Instead of the orderly, well-regulated house of sisters, with a recognised authority and a rule, here there might arise, in the most remote and solitary wilderness, a small wattled oratory, with a single, simple saint living within it, a saint in the old dispensation, without benefit of Pope or canonisation, who grew a few vegetables and herbs for her food, and gathered berries and wild fruit, and came to loving terms with the small beasts of the warren, so that they ran to hide in her skirts when they were hunted, and neither huntsmen not horn could urge on the hounds to do the lady affront, or her little visitors harm. (p.116)

Such a cell, dedicated to St Nonna, mother of St David, whose sacred wells give healing to the eyes, briefly provides shelter for the beautiful and headstrong Heledd, a runaway from an arranged marriage that she does not welcome.

Another, less attractive aspect of Welsh life which Mark and Cadfael encounter, and which leads them into a situation of considerable danger, is the rivalry and enmity between Owain, Prince of Gynnedd, and his brother, Cadwaladr. As the two Benedictines advance into Wales to deliver their second message of support to the Bishop of Bangor they become unexpectedly involved in this feud, which has brought Cadwaladr from Dublin with a fleet of Danish ships and an army of warriers bent on pillage and reward. In the circumstances the murder of an emissary from the enemy camp in Owain's castle at Aber might appear to be of little significance, but Owain regards the crime as an affront to his honour, and pledges to punish the murderer. Brother Mark completes his mission to Bangor, but he and Cadfael feel it their duty to search for the missing girl, Heledd, especially since the Danes are known to be near the coast of Anglesey. The raiders are nearer than they expect, and Cadfael and Heledd are taken prisoner.

The Summer of the Danes carries a glow of summer skies and wide spaces with many loving descriptions of the flat, open plains beneath the slopes of Snowdon and sand dunes lit by the brilliance of the encircling sea. The concerns of bishops and ecclesiastical politics are forgotten as Owain and Cadwaladr, with the Danish captain Otir, contest their claims. Owain's power is triumphant and a resolution is reached with a minimum of bloodshed. The solution to the murder of Bledri is almost incidental to the larger issues of state which are arrived at during this clash of formidable enemies. Heledd finds a romantic future of her own choosing and Cadfael and Mark turn their mounts eastwards towards England with the hope that Owain and his brother may soon reach some kind of reconciliation.

The novel has gone farther than any other of the Cadfael series to bring in the qualities of the highly-regarded history sagas to which Peters devoted many years during the 1960s and 1970s. While it novel contains much interesting material and sustains the central characters of Cadfael and Mark, the element of detection is minimal. Close reasoning and a conflict of wits are therefore all the more welcome in the next novel, *The Holy Thief*, although this novel also deals with a wide political canvas.

The Holy Thief (1992) inherits much of its savour from the first Chronicle, *A Morbid Taste for Bones*, which establishes Cadfael's secret and brings the reader into his confidence about the actual contents of St Winifred's reliquary. The components of the plot are not unfamiliar: a traveller is waylaid and killed on a forest path; a young man is suspected of murder; the real criminal is accused in the abbey courtyard and flees in the direction of Wales; romance finds its way at the end. We are surprised by the sudden violence manifested by Brother Jerome, who up to now has appeared to be no more than a harmless, sanctimonious busybody. Apart from this rather unprepared and uncharacteristic behaviour the murder and its solution follows a fairly predictable route. Other issues appear to be of more interest to the author in this novel, in particular the political state of England and the whole concept of sacred relics and their importance to religious life.

St Winifred's sealed reliquary would probably have rested quite happily on the altar of her chapel in the abbey for many years without being moved had not the river Severn, swollen with rain and melting snow from the mountains of Wales, flooded its banks at Shrewsbury and crept relentlessly across the abbey grounds until it lapped at the pillars in the nave of the church itself. The power of the Severn in flood is constantly present for Peters; from childhood she has been thrilled and alarmed by the sudden changes possible in a river which normally flows peacefully through quiet pastures near the town. In *The Holy Thief* the monks are forced to carry all valuables, indeed anything that can be lifted, to lofts and high chambers where they will be safe. Last to be carried out of the church is the silver-chased reliquary. Its disappearance, its finding and the consequent wrangling over its return to the abbey provide the author with an opportunity to extend further her questioning of the role of faith and its meaning. Differing views are set out one day when Cadfael is sitting with Hugh Beringar and his wife Aline, describing the events in the abbey when three contenders open the bible at random to seek support for their claim to St Winifred, and a mysterious wind turns the pages unaided. 'Too many miracles for one morning!', claims Hugh mischievously. But Cadfael, taking the safe position, leaves some room for belief, saying that 'Miracles...may be simply divine manipulation of ordinary circumstances. Why not?' For Aline, it is a matter of simple faith: 'it is only that the step from perfectly ordinary things into the miraculous seems to me so small, almost accidental, that I wonder why it astonishes you at all, or why you trouble to reason about it. If it were reasonable it could not be miraculous, could it?' Whatever the justification for events, St Winifred's reliquary, but not of course her actual bones, comes back to Shrewsbury, accompanied by a great deal of pomposity from the rival claimant of the Abbey of Ramsey, and considerable witty baiting from the third contender, Earl Robert of Leicester.

Earl Robert is introduced to the Chronicles for the first time and provides valuable insights into the position of England in 1145. In a private and frank conversation Hugh Beringar and the Earl discuss the future. Hugh deplores the waste that civil war has created: 'waste of lives, waste of time that could be profitable, waste of the earth that could be fruitful.' Robert's family is a microcosm of the conflict, with his twin brother in Normandy defending his lands there and inevitably being linked to the empress, and Robert holding the English lands for King Stephen. He shares his honest conclusion with Hugh that 'this has become a war which cannot be won or lost. Victory and defeat have become alike impossible. Unfortunately it may take several years yet before most men begin to understand. We who are trying to ride two horses know it already.' Their conversation ends on a note of mutual respect, and a recognition that for the present there was nothing for a wise man to do but keep his own counsel and manage his own estates. Earl Robert is right to be pessimistic about the immediate future. Not until Matilda's son Henry invaded from Normandy in 1152 did any chance of peace arise. Matilda had ceded her claim to the throne to Henry, and at last a peace was negotiated by Henry, the Bishop of Winchester and the Archbishop of Canterbury to allow Stephen to reign unopposed for the rest of his life, with Henry succeeding him as heir. In 1154 Stephen, the last of the Norman Kings, died and Henry II became monarch. His long and fruitful reign united England and brought the peace and prosperity that had been sought for so long. His good government established him as one of England's greatest kings.

Both *The Summer of the Danes* and *The Holy Thief* bring glimpses into the outside world that are welcome in a series that previously benefited from domestic detail and scrupulous development of a small group of characters and a limited area of action. The twentieth chronicle, *Brother Cadfael's Penance*, continues this trend, taking Cadfael far away from the comforting enclosure of the abbey in Shrewsbury and into the wider world of political struggle, reflecting Peters's deep interest in the historical background to the series and also bringing us closer to the mind of Cadfael as he becomes aware of his increasing years.

The chronology has moved on to late 1145 yet there is still no sign of an end to the conflict between King Stephen and the Empress Maud. The power of the Church is used to attempt a reconciliation by drawing all the contenders to a conference at Coventry. Instrumental in achieving this are Roger de Clinton, the wise and influential Bishop of Coventry, and the Earl of Leicester, Robert Beaumont, who was last encountered in *The Holy Thief*, deep in private conversation with Hugh Beringar about the desperate need for peace in the land.

Civil war is the most cruel of all conflicts, placing son against father, brother against brother. This aspect of the conflict is brought to the foreground in *Brother Cadfael's Penance* where the focus is firmly placed on family ties wrenched apart by war. The duties of parents towards their children are explored in several ways and unexpectedly Cadfael finds himself responsible for rescuing his own son, Olivier de Bretagne, from imprisonment. A different kind of duty leads to murder at the conference in Coventry; the result of an elderly mother's well-considered vengeance for her son's betrayal. The bitter quarrel between Earl Robert of Gloucester, who failed to send men to his son's aid earlier in the summer and whose son abandons his allegiance to the empress as a result, is eventually reconciled. 'Blood is blood', says Olivier, and clearly comes before vows of allegiance to king or empress.

And what is the role of Brother Cadfael in all these affairs of state? Surely he, as a Benedictine brother, sworn to leave his previous life behind as he enters the abbey door, surely he could not be permitted to embark on a quest to find his son? Abbot Radulfus is sufficiently enlightened to send Cadfael with Hugh to Coventry in the hope that information about Olivier might emerge among the company there but he does not give permission for further time away. Yet he knows, as does Cadfael, that his unconventional brother will sacrifice every-thing for Olivier: 'While Olivier went free and fearless and blessed about the world, his father needed nothing more. But Olivier in captivity, stolen out of the world, hidden from the light, that was not to be borne. The darkened void where he had been was an offence against truth.' Cadfael feels that he has a necessary role to play that no one else can fulfill, as 'the pivot at the centre', and he does not shirk the burden, painful though it is to say farewell to Hugh, who is returning to Shrewsbury, and to set off on a journey of his own:

> It was like the breaking of a tight constriction which had bound his life safely within him, though at the cost of pain; and the abrupt removal of the restriction was mingled relief and terror, both intense. The ease of being loose in the world came first, and only gradually did the horror of the release enter and overwhelm him. For he was recreant, he had exiled himself, knowing well what he was doing.

Peters now turns her attention to matters of war and the mechanics of a siege. Although stone castles may appear to be impregnable even the crude devices available to twelfth century soldiers were highly effective, such as fire arrows laden with molten tar, battering rams and mangonels (catapults). Cadfael, naturally, is at the heart of things. Not only does his intervention free Olivier, he indirectly manages to prevent the empress from an act of unwise vindictive-ness that would seriously have affected her position and made peace even more difficult to achieve.

His mission accomplished, Cadfael begins his long and difficult journey back to Shrewsbury, a journey that is full of mental anguish. Winter is at its height and snow followed by floods make the five days of travel into a penitential exercise. All the while he is debating within his mind the painful dilemma that engulfs him. He knows that in the eyes of the church he has sinned. Yet he knows also that he would take the same course again, and he does not repent. Prostrating himself at the entrance to the choir in the cold and deserted abbey church Cadfael is comforted by a dream or even a vision of Saint Winifred reaching towards him. Abbot Radulfus accepts him and his actions as 'an earnest of grace' and Cadfael gratefully takes back his place in the brotherhood: 'all the more to be desired was this order and tranquillity within the pale, where the battle of heaven and hell was fought without bloodshed, with the weapons of the mind and the soul.'

Many readers will welcome the broader canvas of *Brother Cadfael's Penance*, with its concern for the individual involved in issues that can affect the course of history. They will welcome also the development of Brother Cadfael as an aging but still highly effective character who feels that positive results need to be brought about by human efforts, not by pious hopes. It is a more serious novel than many, without the familiar ingredients of romantic attachments and the intimate surroundings of city and abbey. Cadfael's wisdom and Olivier's bravery are a strong combination and may well affect other affairs of state in the future.

The achievement of writing twenty novels in a series without losing the loyal, not to say fanatic, devotion of her huge readership says a great deal about Peters's novelistic skills. These finely-crafted books all ask important questions as to human conduct in society and how we make judgements about one another. As with the worthiest practitioners in this genre, Peters provides serious fiction with a delicate touch; fiction that crosses the boundaries of age, of race, of continent. Brother Cadfael, like Sherlock Holmes, has acquired an identity beyond the pages of fiction, and exists now as a comforting presence for good, a necessary refuge for readers who, like Peters herself, still aspire to optimism about our future.

Conclusion

Many writers, musicians and painters have discovered the creative possibilities of life on the Borders. A special brilliance of light and a landscape defined by hills are physical attractions. Less tangible, yet no less imperative, is the sense of history held in that landscape, a force that has always directed Edith Pargeter's books. She writes in *Shropshire* that:

> To stand alone on top of any of the western hills of Shropshire is to look round on an apparently unpeopled world, and yet it is there that you may suddenly experience this conviction of having a place in a continuity of tenure of this earth that makes you securely one in a chain longer than history. (p.27)

For Pargeter the past is both a heritage and a responsibility. In the introduction to *Cadfael Country* she tells us that to her, in Shropshire, 'the unbroken thread of life and worship persists in the very soil, and reminds us that we are the custodians of this earth, the inheritors of its history and the trustees of its future.'

A writer who has spent a long lifetime in one place, as this author has done, acquires a very special relationship with the landscape and its people. In almost all of her mature fiction, whether contemporary detective novels, historical sagas or the Cadfael Chronicles, the presence of the border between England and Wales has been a generic feature, creating and directing narrative and characterisation.

From the particular, comes the universal, and so it has been in Edith Pargeter's work. At the climax of her professional career as a writer she has achieved not only great popular success but the continuing respect of her peers. The Chronicles of Brother Cadfael have been published in twenty different countries so far and in eighteen languages besides English. Brother Cadfael is likely to remain a formidable presence in Shrewsbury and the Borders for some time to come.

Select Bibliography

WORKS BY EDITH PARGETER

Fiction

Hortensius, Friend of Nero (London, 1936; New York, 1937)
Iron-Bound (London, 1936)
Day Star as by Peter Benedict (London, 1937)
Murder in the Dispensary, as by Jolyon Carr, (London, 1938)
The City Lies Foursquare (London and New York, 1939)
Freedom For Two as by Jolyon Carr (London, 1939)
Masters of the Parachute Mail as by Jolyon Carr (London, 1940)
Death Comes by Post as by Jolyon Carr (London, 1940)
The Victim Needs a Nurse as by John Redfern (London, 1940)
Ordinary People (London 1941; as *People of My Own,* New York, 1942)
She Goes to War (London, 1942)
The Eighth Champion of Christendom (London, 1945)
Reluctant Odyssey (London, 1946)
Warfare Accomplished (London, 1947)
The Fair Young Phoenix (London, 1948)
By Firelight (London, 1948; as *By This Strange Fire,* New York, 1948)
Lost Children (London, 1951)
Holiday with Violence (London, 1952)
This Rough Magic (London, 1953)
Most Loving Mere Folly (London, 1953)
The Soldier at the Door (London, 1954)
A Means of Grace (London, 1956)
Death Mask (London, 1959; New York, 1960)
The Will and the Deed (London, 1960; as *Where There's a Will,* New York, 1960)

141

EDITH PARGETER: ELLIS PETERS

The Heaven Tree (London and New York, 1960)
The Green Branch (London, 1962)
The Scarlet Seed (London, 1963)
Funeral of Figaro (London, 1962; New York, 1964)
A Bloody Field by Shrewsbury (London, 1972; New York, 1973)
The Horn of Roland (London and New York, 1974)
Sunrise in the West (London, 1974)
The Dragon at Noonday (London, 1975)
The Hounds of Sunset (London, 1976)
Afterglow and Nightfall (London, 1977)
Never Pick Up Hitch-Hikers! (London and New York, 1976)
The Marriage of Meggotta (London and New York, 1979)

The Felse Novels (all as by Ellis Peters except where noted)

Fallen into the Pit, published as Edith Pargeter (London, 1951)
Death and the Joyful Woman (London, 1961; New York, 1962)
Flight of a Witch (London, 1964)
A Nice Derangement of Epitaphs (London, 1965; as *Who Lies Here*
　　New York, 1965)
The Piper on the Mountain (London and New York, 1966)
Black is the Colour of My True-Love's Heart (London and New York, 1967)
The Grass-Widow's Tale (London and New York, 1968)
The House of Green Turf (London and New York, 1969)
Mourning Raga (London, 1969, New York, 1970)
The Knocker on Death's Door (London, 1970; New York, 1971)
Death to the Landlords! (London and New York, 1972)
City of Gold and Shadows (London, 1973; New York, 1974)
Rainbow's End (London, 1978; New York, 1979)

The Chronicles of Brother Cadfael (all as by Ellis Peters)

A Morbid Taste for Bones: A Mediaeval Whodunnit (London, 1977;
　　New York, 1978)
One Corpse Too Many (London, 1979; New York, 1980)
Monk's-Hood (London, 1980; New York, 1981)
Saint Peter's Fair (London and New York, 1981)

SELECT BIBLIOGRAPHY

The Leper of Saint Giles (London, 1981; New York, 1982)
The Virgin in the Ice (London 1982; New York, 1983)
The Sanctuary Sparrow (London and New York, 1983)
The Devil's Novice (London 1983; New York, 1984)
Dead Man's Ransom (London and New York, 1984)
The Pilgrim of Hate (London and New York, 1984)
An Excellent Mystery (London, 1985; New York, 1986)
The Raven in the Foregate (London and New York, 1986)
The Rose Rent (London and New York, 1986)
The Hermit of Eyton Forest (London, 1987; New York, 1988)
The Confession of Brother Haluin (London, 1988; New York, 1989)
The Heretic's Apprentice (London, 1989; New York, 1990)
The Potter's Field (London, 1989; New York, 1990)
The Summer of the Danes (London and New York,1991)
The Holy Thief (London, 1992; New York, 1993)
Brother Cadfael's Penance (London and New York, 1994)

Short Story Collections

The Assize of the Dying (London and New York, 1958)
The Lily Hand and Other Stories (London, 1965)
A Rare Benedictine, published as by Ellis Peters (London, 1988; New
    York, 1989)

Non-fiction Books

The Coast of Bohemia (London, 1950)
Shropshire, with Roy Morgan (Stroud, 1992)
Strongholds and Sanctuaries, with Roy Morgan (Stroud, 1993)

Essay (as by Ellis Peters)

'The Thriller is a Novel', in *Techniques of Novel-Writing*, edited by
    A.S. Burack (Boston, 1973)

Translations from Czech (all as Edith Pargeter)

Tales of the Little Quarter: Stories, by Jan Neruda (London, 1957; New York, 1976)
The Sorrowful and Heroic Life of John Amos Comenius, by Frantisek Kozik (Prague, 1958)
A Handful of Linden Leaves: An Anthology of Czech Poetry (Prague, 1958)
Don Juan, by Josef Toman (London and New York, 1958)
The Abortionists, by Valja Styblova (London, 1961)
Granny, by Bozena Nemcova (Prague, 1962; New York, 1976)
The Linden Tree, anthology, with others (Prague, 1962)
The Terezin Requiem, by Josef Bor (London and New York, 1963)
Legends of Old Bohemia, by Alois Jirasek (London, 1963)
The Wolf Trap, by Jarmila Glazarova (Prague, 1963)
May, by Karel Hynek Macha (Prague, 1965)
The End of the Old Times, by Vladislav Vancura (Prague, 1965)
A Close Watch on the Trains, by Bohumil Hrabal (London, 1968)
Report on My Husband, by Josefa Slanska (London, 1969)
A Ship Named Hope, by Ivan Klima (London, 1970)
Mozart in Prague, by Jaroslav Seifert (Prague, 1970)

REFERENCE WORKS

Books

Baugh, G.C. and Cox, D.C., *Monastic Shropshire*, revised edition (Shrewsbury, 1988)
Binyon,T.J., *'Murder Will Out': The Detective in Fiction* (Oxford, 1989).
Cawelti, John G., *Adventure, Mystery and Romance* (Chicago, 1976).
Davies, John, *A History of Wales*, English edition (London, 1993).
Davis, R.H.C., A *History of Medieval Europe*, fifth impression (London, 1991).
Twentieth Century Crime and Mystery Writers, edited by L. Henderson, third edition (Chicago, 1991).
McEwan, Neil, *Perspectives in British Historical Fiction Today* (London, 1987).

SELECT BIBLIOGRAPHY

Paul, David W., *Czechoslovakia: Profile of a Socialist Republic at the Crossroads of Europe* (Boulder, Colorado, 1981).

Smith, Goldwin, *A History of England* (New York, 1957).

Symons, Julian, *Bloody Murder*, revised edition (London 1985).

Talbot, Rob and Whitehouse, Robin, *Cadfael Country* (1990).

Ulc, Otto, *Politics in Czechoslovakia* (San Francisco, 1974).

White, Patrick, *Flaws in the Glass* (London, 1981).

Sharon L Wolchik, *Czechoslovakia in Transition: Politics, Economics and Society* (London, 1991).

Articles and Essays

Ashley, Mike, 'Mistress of the Medieval Mystery', *Million*, (July-August 1991) 6-11.

Christian, Edwin Ernest and Lindsey, Blake, 'The Habit of Detection: The Medieval Monk as Detective in the Novels of Ellis Peters', *Studies in Medievalism*, IV (1992) 276-289.

Cooke, Catherine, 'The Chronicles of Brother Cadfael: A Pilgrim's Testament', *CADS 9* (July 1988) 3-12.

Feder, Sue, editor, *Most Loving Mere Folly*, 1-23 (Maryland).

Feder, Sue, 'Ellis Peters' in *Twentieth Century Crime and Mystery Writers*, edited by L. Henderson, third edition (Chicago, 1991) 846-849.

Greeley, Andrew M., 'Ellis Peters: another Umberto Eco?', *The Armchair Detective*, 18:3 (Summer 1985) 238-245.

Gwilt, J.R., 'Brother Cadfael's Herbiary', *The Pharmaceutical Journal* (December 19/26, 1992) 807-809.

Harriot, John F.X., 'Detective Extraordinary', *The Tablet* , 240: 7631 (11 October 1986) 1066.

Herbert, Rosemary, 'PW Interviews — Ellis Peters', *Publishers' Weekly* (August 9, 1991) 40-41.

Hodge, Jane Aiken, 'Writing Historical Novels', in *Techniques of Novel Writing*, edited by A.S. Burack, (Boston, 1973) 219-224.

Parrott, Sir Cecil, 'Czechoslovakia — its heritage and its future', 47th Earl Grey Memorial Lecture, published by the University of Newcastle upon Tyne, 1968.

Ryan, Kathleen, 'Holes and Flaws in Medieval Irish Manuscripts', *Peritha, 6-7 (1987-88)* 243-264.

Rudolph, Janet A., ed 'Religious Mysteries' Issue, *Mystery Readers Journal*, 8:3 (Fall 1992).

Shideler, Mary McDermott, 'The Whodunnit is Fiction's Most Moral Genre', *Books and Religion*, 15:5 (Fall 1987) 11-14.

The Times, 25 May, 1993, 'The Battle of the Atlantic Supplement', I-XVI

Vinson, James and Kirkpatrick, D.L., (eds) *Contemporary Novelists*, third edition (London, 1982) 728.

Interviews

'The Prime Crimes of Ellis Peters' [with Sarah Booth Conroy], *The Washington Post*, 28 Sept. 1991, 3-4.

'Murder Medieval' [tape recorded interview with Barbara Peters], The Poisoned Pen Bookshop, Scottsdale, Arizona, 16 March 1993

'Murder is Her Habit' [with Stephen Pile], *Telegraph Magazine*, 12 October 1991, 51-54.

'Ellis Peters' [with June E. Prance], *British Digest Illustrated*, Spring 1993, 15-17.

'The Green Detective' [with Dana Wynter], *The Guardian*, 22 November 1989.

Series Afterword

The Border country is that region between England and Wales which is upland and lowland, both and neither. Centuries ago kings and barons fought over these Marches without their national allegience ever being settled. In our own time, referring to his childhood, that eminent borderman Raymond Williams once said: 'We talked of "The English" who were not us, and "The Welsh" who were not us.' It is beautiful, gentle, intriguing and often surprising. It displays majestic landscapes, which show a lot, and hide some more. People now walk it, poke into its cathedrals and bookshops, and fly over or hang-glide from its mountains, yet its mystery remains.

In cultural terms the region is as fertile as (in parts) its agriculture and soil. The continued success of the Three Choirs Festival and the growth of the border town of Hay as a centre of the secondhand book trade have both attracted international recognition. The present series of introductory books is offered in the light of such events. Writers as diverse as Mary Webb, Raymond Williams and Wilfred Owen are seen in the special light — perhaps that cloudy, golden twilight so characteristic of the region — of their origin in this area or association with it. There are titles too, though fewer, on musicians and painters. The Gloucestershire composers such as Samuel Sebastian Wesley, and painters like David Jones, bear an imprint of border woods, rivers, villages and hills.

How wide is the border? Two, five or fifteen miles each side of the boundary; it depends on your perspective, on the placing of the nearest towns, on the terrain itself, and on history. In the time of Offa and after, Hereford itself was a frontier town, and Welsh was spoken there even in the nineteenth century. True border folk traditionally did not recognize those from even a few miles away. Today, with greater mobility, the crossing of boundaries is easier, whether for education, marriage, art or leisure. For myself, who spent some childhood years in Herefordshire and a decade of middle-age crossing between England and Wales once a week, I can only say that as you approach the border you feel it. Suddenly you are in that finally elusive terrain, looking from a bare height down onto the plain, or from the lower land up to a gap in the hills, and you want to explore it, maybe not to return.

This elusiveness pertains to the writers and artists too. It is often difficult to decide who is border, to what extent and with what impact on their work. The urbane Elizabeth Barrett Browning, prominent figure of the salons of London and Italy in her time, spent virtually all her life until her late twenties outside Ledbury in Herefordshire, and this fact is being seen by current critics and scholars as of more and more significance. The twentieth century 'English pastoral' composers — with names like Parry, Howells, and Vaughan Williams — were nearly all border people. One wonders whether border country is now suddenly found on the English side of the Severn Bridge, and how far even John Milton's *Comus*, famous for its first production in Ludlow Castle, is in any sense such a work. Then there is the fascinating Uxbridge-born Peggy Whistler, transposed in the 1930s into Margiad Evans to write her (epilepsis-based) visionary novels set near her adored Ross-on-Wye and which today still retain a magical charm. Further north: could Barbara Pym, born and raised in Oswestry, even remotely be called a border writer? Most people would say that the poet A.E. Housman was far more so, yet he hardly ever visited the county after which his chief book of poems, *A Shropshire Lad*, is named. Further north still: there is the village of Chirk on the boundary itself, where R.S. Thomas had his first curacy; there is Gladstone's Hawarden Library, just outside Chester and actually into Clwyd in Wales itself; there is intriguingly the Wirral town of Birkenhead, where Wilfred Owen spent his adolescence and where his fellow war poet Hedd Wyn was awarded his Chair — posthumously.

On the Welsh side the names are different. The mystic Ann Griffiths; the metaphysical poet Henry Vaughan; the astonishing nineteenth century symbolist novelist Arthur Machen (in Linda Dowling's phrase, 'Pater's prose as registered by Wilde'); and the remarkable Thomas Olivers of Gregynog, associated with the writing of the well-known hymn 'Lo He comes with clouds descending'. Those descending clouds...; in border country the scene hangs overhead, and it is easy to indulge in unwarranted speculation. Most significant perhaps is the difference to the two peoples on either side. From England, the border meant the enticement of emptiness, a strange unpopulated land, going up and up into the hills. From Wales, the border meant the road to London, to the university, or to employment, whether by droving sheep, or later to the industries of Birmingham and Liverpool. It also meant the enemy, since borders and boundaries are necessarily political. Much is shared, yet different languages are spoken, in more than one sense.

With certain notable exceptions, the books in this series are short introductory studies of one person's work or some aspect of it. There are nofootnote or indexes. The bibliography lists main sources referred to in the text and sometimes others, for anyone who would like to pursue the topic further. The authors reflect the diversity of their subjects. They are specialists or academics; critics or biographers; poets or musicians themselves; or ordinary people with, however, an established reputation of writing imaginatively and directly about what moves them. They are of various ages, both sexes, Welsh and English, border people themselves or from further afield.

To those who explore the matter, the subjects — the writers, painters and composers written about — seem increasingly united by a particular kind of vision. This holds good however diverse they are in other, main ways; and of course they are diverse indeed. One might scarcely associate, it would seem, Raymond Williams with Samuel Sebastian Wesley, or Dennis Potter with Thomas Traherne. But one has to be careful in such assumptions. The epigraph to Bruce Chatwin's twentieth century novel *On the Black Hill* is a passage from the seventeenth century mystic writer Jeremy Taylor. Thomas Traherne himself is the subject of a recent American study which puts Traherne's writings into dialogue with the European philosopher-critics Martin Heidegger, Jacques Derrida and Jacques Lacan. And a current bestselling writer of thrillers, Ellis Peters, sets her stories in a Shrewsbury of the late medieval Church with a cunning quiet monk as her ever-engaging sleuth.

The vision (name incidentally of the farmhouse in Chatwin's novel) is something to do with the curious border light already mentioned. To avoid getting sentimental and mystic here — though border writers have at times been both — one might suggest literally that this effect is meteorological. Maybe the sun's rays are refracted through skeins of dew or mist that hit the stark mountains and low hills at curious ascertainable angles, with prismatic results. Not that rainbows are the point in our area: it is more the contrasts of gold green and grey. Some writers never mention it. They don't have to But all the artists of the region see it, are affected by it, and transpose their highly different emanations of reality through its transparencies. Meanwhile, on the ground, the tourist attractions draw squads from diverse cultural and ethnic origins; agriculture enters the genetic-engineering age; New Age travellers are welcome and unwelcome; and the motorway runs up parallel past all — 'Lord of the M5', as the poet Geoffrey Hill has dubbed the Saxon king Offa, he of the dyke which bisects the region where it can still be identified. The region has its uniqueness, then, and a statistically above-average number of writers and artists (we have identified over fifty clear candidates so far) have drawn something from it, which it is the business of this present series to elucidate.

In the long late section of the present pioneering study, Margaret Lewis has included a critical summary — without betrayals — of every single one of the twenty-plus Cadfael Chronicles already in existence. It is indeed fascinating that this authentically and explicitly border writer raises all the current questions about the detective thriller as literary genre. Yet the millions of Ellis Peters followers in Britain and around the world may not realise that her total published books number more than three times those of the Cadfael series, that they include a war trilogy and a history trilogy, and that their author has enjoyed a happy and fruitful relationship with the country of Czechoslovakia all her adult life. Her several expertises as novelist, mystery writer and medieval historian ensure her pre-eminent attention at a time when literary boundaries are breaking down and new forms are emerging.

John Powell Ward

The Author

Margaret Lewis was born in Northern Ireland and educated at the universities of Alberta, Leeds and Newcastle upon Tyne. She is a writer and a contributor to public relations at the University of Newcastle upon Tyne. In addition to her short stories broadcast on the radio and published in anthologies, she is the author of the biobgraphy *Ngaio Marsh: A Life* (Chatto, 1991).